Memories of a Country Girlhood

Memories of a Country Girlhood

A Trilogy — Part 1

Ellen Smith

Memories of a Country Girlhood
Ellen Smith

First edition published by author 1983.

Second edition published by Heart of Albion Press
on behalf of Wymeswold Church Appeal Fund 2005.

ISBN 1 872883 86 9

Illustrations by Susan Jalland
Cover and title page by Gaynor Smith

Heart of Albion Press
2 Cross Hill Close, Wymeswold
Loughborough, LE12 6UJ

albion@indigogroup.co.uk

Visit our Web site: www.hoap.co.uk

Printed in England by Booksprint

*To my much loved brother
John Wootton
and my sincere thanks to my son David
without whose help this book
would never have been published.*

Contents

FOREWORD

At the age of seventy-three years I decided to look back over my long and busy life and to write about my experiences in the village of Wymeswold where I was born and have lived all my life. My parents and grandparents spent all their lives here and so have two of my three brothers. I have known five generations of my family who have carried on a building business in and around this village – my grandfather, father, brothers, nephew and great-nephew. I married into a family who has farmed in the village for at least five generations. Two of my sons and one grandson are farmers, following in the footsteps of my husband, his father and his grandfather. In my childhood most members of the community were farmers or were connected with farming. Almost all the land, including the vicarage, was owned by Trinity College, Cambridge, but it was sold in 1955 to the tenants. The college still maintains the chancel in the village church of St Mary's.

When I was young, the village was quite self-contained: we produced almost all the things we needed, including entertainment. The population was then a little over six hundred, but as with most close-knit villages, changes have taken place and the population has doubled, necessitating many more dwellings, but basically the village has retained its old image. Life centred round the school, the beautiful, old church, the Wesleyan and Baptist chapels and, after World War I, the village hall, built in memory of the fallen.

I am not writing these memoirs for want of something to do. Since the death of my husband fourteen years ago, my only daughter and I have built up a poultry business with some 7000 laying hens, selling all our eggs on market stalls. The incentive was provided by the pleasure my stories seem to give my grandchildren. So often one or another would say: "That ought to be written down, grandma." Many of my family and friends thought the same, especially my friend and workmate Susan Jalland, who has typed the manuscript and illustrated this book, and my granddaughter Gaynor, who has designed the title page. Their encouragement and enthusiasm have been of immense help to me.

My education has been minimal, as I left school at the age of thirteen, but I shall endeavour to leave my fourteen grandchildren an authentic account of my childhood and their ancestors' way of life in this lovely village, the gradual changes which have taken place there, the trials and tribulations of farming, and above all the wonderful happiness of my family life.

Wymeswold, 8 January 1982

1 THE VILLAGE

My native village of Wymeswold nestles in a valley on the wolds in the north-east corner of Leicestershire. In the centre of the village the beautiful church of St Mary's stands on a rise overlooking the village square. The church is very large for a village of less than a thousand inhabitants. I have often heard it called the cathedral of English village churches. It was built in the Middle Ages but was restored by Dean Alford in the nineteenth century. On the other side of the square stands the Church of England School. The church and the school were the pivot of most of the social life of the village. The infants' school was further up the Far Street but is now a dwelling-house.

The Methodist Chapel stands in the Stockwell and still has a good congregation. The Baptist Chapel was built just outside the village on the Wysall Lane but was sold in the 1950s because of the dwindling congregation. This chapel is now a dwelling-house, standing in the middle of a graveyard.

The Post Office and shop is situated on the east side of the church and has been run as long as I can remember by the Brown family. Its owner, Mr Philip Brown, was the only man in the village who could take photographs, which he developed and printed in sepia. Sometimes at the village parties he would show these photographs in lantern-shows. We children would love sitting in the dark waiting for the next slide and usually there would be someone we knew on each of them. These old films are extremely valuable now. His granddaughter, Miss Joy Brown, who now owns the Post Office, occasionally allows these slides to be shown on an old lantern projector in the village hall. These films are very much appreciated by both old and new residents.

In Brook Street there was the largest shop in the village, run by Mr Thomas Brown, brother to Mr Philip Brown. This shop, now converted into two houses, sold groceries, shoes and drapery. Brook Street is so called because of the brook running through the centre of the road, called the River Mantle, which frequently burst its banks. One August day there was a cloudburst and it rained steadily all day, causing the brook to flood. In spite of sandbags some houses in Brook Street were flooded. Boats were rowed on the deep waters of the street. The water gradually crept out of the village and down the Hoton Road, eventually flooding a field where a farmer kept a lot of hens. Our family was marooned in our house and we watched the hens being rescued. Now a new culvert and pipes have been laid; heavy rain water is soon dispersed into the brook beyond the village and there has been no recurrence of bad floods. In the hens' field several new houses have now been built.

The third shop was in our street, called Clay Street, and was kept by Miss Wood and her niece, Miss Simpson. Miss Wood had been a lifelong friend of my Wootton grandparents and Miss Simpson was one of my parents' best friends. The shop sold many things. When one entered the door, one was in the grocery department. The room itself would not measure more than twelve feet across and certainly not more than fifteen feet long. There was a wooden counter with brass scales and weights, always highly polished, which were used for weighing sweets and small things. Another set further along the counter, made of copper and much bigger, was used for weighing lard, sugar, cheese, bacon, etc. Next to the cheese and bacon table was a huge red tank from which paraffin was sold. No one was allowed to serve this paraffin but Miss Simpson, in case they were careless and a spot of paraffin fell on the cheese and bacon counter. This arrangement would never be allowed these days.

The shop window was only a yard and a half wide and perhaps one yard in height, so we children had to stand on tiptoe to look at the sweets, which were kept in huge glass jars on shelves inside the window. We never had any pocket money and were never given any until we went out to work at the age of thirteen. Sometimes one of the representatives who called to sell building materials to father would give us a sixpence each – a sprat to catch a mackerel, I suppose. Then it would be "corn in Egypt". We would troop to the little shop and choose a farthing's worth of one sort of sweet and another farthing on a different sort and the rest was put away in our money boxes. Mother always made us save: if we had one penny given to us, a halfpenny went into our money boxes. A treat on Saturday nights came from father, who always brought half a pound of sweets to share between us, and these were usually divided two at a time every morning until they were gone.

The other part of the shop sold drapery, anything from cottons, pins and needles to underclothing and flannelette by the yard. At Christmas the drapery window would be resplendent with toys, quite inexpensive toys but far beyond the means of some of the poorer families in the village. The village kids congregated around this window many weeks before Christmas, gazing with rapt eyes, hoping they might be lucky enough to have at least one toy for Christmas. Over the shop were three rooms, one for storage and another for the sale of boots and shoes. The third room was used for dressmaking. Miss Wood and Miss Simpson spent their spare time making dresses for most of the village ladies; all my mother's and our four girls' dresses were made here. When I grew older and saw some of the work they used to do, I was amazed at the tremendous amount of sewing that went into making one dress and I wondered how in the world two ladies managed a shop of this kind and still did such a lot of beautiful sewing. These ladies were so kind that, if the children of poor families had no shoes, they would fit them out from old stock, even though the parents concerned owed them a large grocery bill. I knew one family with ten children, who all benefited in turn from their generosity.

There were also two small shops, one in the village square, under the shadow of the church, and the other in Far Street. The first is now one of the three grocer's in the village, the second is a small antique shop next to where the James family had their petrol pumps. All these shops in a village with only 600 residents seemed quite a lot, but they all made a living.

My auntie Sarah once sent me to the shop in the square for several articles and she recited to me the things she needed, adding at the end "a pennyiower". I could not think what this was, but I asked for a pennyiower just the same. As the shopkeeper did not know what it was either, she told me to ask my auntie to write it down. "Good gracious me!" said auntie, "I owe the lady one penny." How a child mistakes the meaning of grown up words. One other funny mistake I made for several years was in the line of a prayer. The phrase "Pity my simplicity" I used to think was "Pity mice implicitly".

There were three butcher's, one of which was run by the James family for three generations. We called them old John James, young John James and young John James's son John James. They also had a meat stall in the Loughborough market every Thursday and Saturday, but now that young John James's son has retired, his sons have taken up farming, so the James's butcher business is no more.

Mr Fred Jalland and his sons, Percy and Harry, ran another butcher's shop in Far Street. They also sold meat from a horse-drawn cart in several of the surrounding villages, later using a van for this purpose. Now Harry's son Roger slaughters animals for customers' deep-freezers, but retailing has been discontinued. Fred Collington's sons and grandsons still run their shop on Far Street, the only butcher's left in the village; they also sell meat in several of the other villages.

There was also a pork-butcher's shop on Brook Street, run by Mr and Mrs Savage. Mr Savage killed the pigs, as many as two or three a week, in the yard behind the shop. His wife made porkpies, sausage, haslet, faggots, black puddings and all sorts of cooked meats. Their shop-window can still be seen: it is part of a thatched cottage next door to what was the village blacksmith's. When Mr and Mrs Savage retired, Wymeswold people were lucky to have the Taylor family living in Clay Street, who started a similar pork butcher's business. In addition to selling in the village, they started a market stall in Loughborough, where Taylor's porkpies became famous. Their son Jim and daughter Winnie were the two who built up a thriving business on their stall. Jim also collected eggs from the village farmers, which his Loughborough customers greatly appreciated. Now they are retired and another local trade has gone.

One other craft that died out was stocking making. An old man named Smith, who lived next door to our builder's yard, had a huge machine that made a dreadful noise, but it was fascinating to watch the stockings appearing down the length of his contraption. When Mr Smith passed away, no other person could work the machine.

The three bakers were Mr Warren Walker, Mr Bartram and Mr Frank Wood. Mrs Wood was a wonderful cook: her puff pastry was renowned in all the surrounding villages in the wolds. After the bread was baked, the villagers would take their own pastry, tarts and pies to be baked in the big oven. Tarts were baked for one penny a dozen. When our father killed a pig, Mrs Wood always baked mother's porkpies for around twopence each. Bread is no longer baked in the village.

At one time there were seven public houses in Wymeswold, but in my lifetime there have been only the present four: the Three Crowns, the White Horse, the Windmill and the Hammer and Pincers.

The blacksmith's shop was in Brook Street. We kids were allowed to watch him shoe the horses, some of which were quiet and didn't seem to mind having their new shoes fitted, but others hated it, making a great fuss. Some would kick out ferociously, bucking and stamping, but Mr Hayes was clever in evading their kicks. It was fascinating to watch Mr Hayes shaping a shoe on his anvil to fit the horse's foot. As the new shoes were applied while they were hot, the hoof smoked and smelled horrible. I always wondered why having nails hammered into their hooves never seemed to hurt them.

There was one shoemaker and one cobbler whose thatched shop stood in the square between the lych gate and the sweet shop. It was considered a great privilege for a child to be allowed to sit and watch Mr Wood's clever fingers sewing the boots and shoes.

Mr Morris was the saddler who made and mended harness. He also kept foxhounds, some of which were so fierce and dangerous, children were scared to death to go near his place. Once one escaped and ran amuck in the infants' playground on the other side of the road. Fortunately Mr Morris arrived in time before much damage was done. This Mr Morris used to get drunk and we children used to watch him from a safe distance. His thatched shop on East Road later became a grocery and newsagent's but is now part of the house next door.

Mr Lamb was the village carpenter, wheelwright and undertaker. Again, we kids were allowed to watch when they were fixing iron rims on wooden wheels. They built a fire with sticks and shavings into the size and shape of a wheel, they left the iron rim on the fire until it reached a certain heat, then the wooden wheel was fixed and hammered into place. The whole wheel was then taken off the fire and water poured over it. The work was very specialized and not always successful. Sometimes I realized something had gone wrong and they had to start all over again.

We also had a cheese factory where all the farmers took their milk, which was made into Stilton cheese. We even had a coal merchant, Mr Savage, who sold coal for one and threepence per hundred-weight.

2 THE FAMILY

My grandparents on both sides lived in the village all their lives and were married in St Mary's Church. My father's parents were Joseph Warner Wootton, a master builder working in Wymeswold and the surrounding villages, and Mary Mills, whose parents were farmers in the village. My mother's parents were William Hardy, a Wymeswold farmer, and Mary Hardy, his first cousin. I do not remember my grandmother Hardy, for she died of diabetes before my mother's marriage. Grandfather Hardy's second wife was a schoolteacher, many years his junior, named Miss Perry. We were taught to call her Perry, never grandma. One of my best memories of Perry was when she invited us to her house for a children's party.

When she got tired of our noise, she used to hand out great pieces of home-made toffee, which was so tacky it stuck to the top of our mouths and closed our teeth together. We had great difficulty in chewing this toffee, but it always had the desired effect of keeping the lot of us quiet. Grandfather Hardy was the vicar's warden for many years. I remember him quite clearly at church services, especially when he came around with the collecting box. My eldest sister remembers him dressed in a frock coat, yellow waistcoat and striped trousers. He wore a beard under his chin, which looked like a frill, but his face was clean-shaven.

Grandfather and Grandma Wootton were both extremely strict with us children in every way. We dared not step into their house without taking off our boots or cleaning them thoroughly, and we always had to wash our hands before sitting down to eat. We girls were made to sit properly in our chairs, never lounge, nor cross our knees or even our feet, and we were constantly ordered to sit with our knees together. We were told always to be ladylike and behave well at home, then we would behave well when we were out. Our

Wootton grandparents were staunch church people, until the church dignitaries wanted to start a raffle in aid of church funds. Grandfather totally disagreed with this form of betting and, after words had been exchanged, he left the church and became a Baptist, his wife and his daughter, our Aunt Sarah, following suit.

In her young days Grandma Wootton, along with her daughters Sarah and Florrie, worked terribly hard. She had a large flock of poultry and a herd of cows which she milked herself. She used to drive into Notting-ham, a matter of twelve miles, to sell the butter and Colwick cheese she had made, along with eggs and poultry which she killed, plucked and dressed. As she got older, she found killing the birds became more difficult, her hands grew weaker and she was unable to do this job thoroughly. One day she asked me to hold a hen while she cut its throat. I shall never forget the long time it seemed to take. I was petrified but dared not refuse to do her bidding. When the gruesome job was done, she sat down on a three-legged milking-stool to pluck the bird. I can still see her in my mind's eye wearing a hessian apron, with a bird on her knee, plucking out its feathers, muttering to herself: "This is the last bird I'll ever kill. Yes, I mean it this time. Never, never again. I've killed hundreds in my time but now I've got to admit it, I'm past it." That was the last bird she ever killed. Grandma spoiled my grandfather terribly. Everything and everybody came second to him. She did many hard jobs that he should have done.

In the 1920s grandma became very ill indeed and, after she had suffered two minor strokes, grandfather employed a housekeeper to look after them both. This arrangement proved very unsatisfactory, so Florrie, my eldest sister, who was still in her teens, gave up her job to look after them. Grandma's condition, known as creeping paralysis, gradually became worse and my mother and Aunt Sarah took turns to sit up at night with her. Several other friends, especially Miss Simpson, the shopkeeper, volunteered to help, relieving them of the odd night or two. After slowly deteriorating over many months, grandma died of a stroke. My sister Florrie was exhausted with the continual nursing of grandma, so grandfather came to live with us, back into the house where he had lived during his young working years. He never really recovered from his wife's death. Although he was quite active, he just faded away. This left us without a grandparent. Grandfather Hardy had died just before this time, but he had been ably looked after by his second wife, Perry.

Perry died a few years afterwards of a malignant growth on her head. Although she was always telling my mother about her intention to make her will, she omitted to do so. She had inherited all my grandfather owned and her nephew, who was unknown to any of grandfather's relations, inherited everything from her, even things that belonged to my mother and all Perry's clothing. Fortunately, Grandmother Hardy had left all her own property in trust to grandfather, so that it came to her children at his death. Grandma Hardy's mother, our great-grandma, had been house-keeper for the Rev John Air, a vicar of Wymeswold, and this gentleman had left her properties and valuable cut glass and silver. The glass and silver my mother divided between her daughters. Some of the properties are now owned by my youngest brother Bill, the others were sold.

My father, Thomas Warner Wootton, was a master builder. Following in his father's footsteps, he built houses for over fifty years in Wymeswold and other places. He was a man with a great sense of humour and a great tease to his family. My mother was the most wonderful woman I have known and the older I get, that opinion grows stronger. Her maiden name was Mary Hardy. My parents spent over fifty extremely happy years together, having seven children, three boys and four girls.

The first child was a boy, who was named Joseph Warner, the second was a girl named Florence Mary, and a third, a girl, they named Lottie. I was the fourth child and was named Ellen. This name was used only when I was in disgrace, otherwise everyone called me Nell. The next was another girl named Edna May, the fifth child in less than eight years of marriage.

Mother very much hoped that this child would be the last, but three and a half years later another boy was born and he was named John. This baby, mother said, was definitely the last, but no, one more boy was yet to come. My eldest brother, Warner, always called him "The Peace-rejoicing baby". Apparently my father took out one of his workmen, who had arrived home safely after four years in the first World War, for a night's celebration. Both men were slightly inebriated on their return home and nine months later mother was delivered of another boy. Four days afterwards the workman's wife also had a son. Our last baby was named William.

We all lived in a three-bedroomed house in Clay Street. It had no bathroom and the closet was twenty yards up the garden. This earth closet had two grown up seats and one child's seat and in those days, especially on dark nights, we visited it in twos and threes. It was not unusual for three of us to perform together in the mornings, otherwise one or two were bound to be late for school, which was a great offence in my young days. There was no toilet paper but small pieces of newspaper hung up on a string. We had no piped water and everything fell into the pit below, which was cleaned out once every year, or a little more often if full. This was then put on the land and ploughed in. In winter the smell was not too bad but in the summer it was just awful. Every child was sent, winter and summer alike, to perform before going to bed. In the winter, sitting on those draughty seats froze one's bottom stiff.

We had a large garden which grew all our vegetables and soft fruits. At the side of this garden was the builder's yard where father kept his store of bricks, roofing tiles, sanitary pipes, etc. Then there were several buildings which housed tools, lime, cement and other things that must not get wet or frosted. Above the yard and garden we had a fine orchard with all kinds of fruit trees and at the top of the orchard were the stables and cart sheds. All this was a children's paradise. I can never remember being bored while we lived at this place.

Father had many horses I remember well. At one time there were a couple of heavy horses which pulled big loads of building materials.

Then we had what was called a dray horse which took the men to the job where they were working and, last but not least, we had a beautiful white pony which my father drove in a high gig. When we children knew that father would be using this pony, we would get up early to see it leave, because after the pony was tackled to the gig, he would not start off until he had gone through the usual pantomime of rearing on his hind legs, time after time, until father gave him a sharp lash of the whip. We all loved this dramatic performance, but mother was relieved when eventually the pony decided to convey father sedately on his journey.

3 CHILDHOOD

The first thing I can remember, although my mother said this was not possible as I was only three years old, was coming in from play one day and finding we could not use the back door. My father and his workmen had taken out the kitchen floor, the old black cooking stove and the old sink. Much to our delight, we were told we must use the front door for the next few days. The front door was used only for special visitors, like the doctor, the vicar and building representatives. A few days later, we were allowed back into our modernized kitchen. Now we had a splendid new stove with an oven on one side and a boiler for heating water on the other. Instead of the rough brick floor, we had red tiles. We also had a beautiful glazed cream sink. After these alterations we started to have breakfast and dinner in the kitchen, except on Sunday when we all went into the dining-living-room, where we could all sit down around a huge mahogany table. In the kitchen three of the middle-sized children had to stand up to eat their meals. We stood between the table and the back wall, which we called the niche (pronounced 'nick'), because of the lack of room for chairs.

My mother had a supreme method of getting through her housework and cooking for a family of nine. On Sunday we always had a nine-pound joint of beef with Yorkshire pudding. Monday we had cold leftover beef and mashed potatoes with pickles and, for pudding, the hated sago or rice.

This was an easy meal for mother because Monday was washday for the white laundry. On Tuesday mother cut up the rest of the meat into small cubes along with potatoes cut in the same way and mixed them together with seasoning and gravy, putting all this into a deep pie dish, with a short crust pastry on top. Mother made the best meat and potato pie I ever tasted. On Wednesday we had a whole leg of mutton, greens and mashed potatoes, with onion sauce spread over it all. Thursday, after a spotted dick pudding, we ate the remains of the mutton with mashed potatoes and pickled onions for those who liked them. Friday mother cooked steak with baked onions and the usual mashed potatoes. I never remember her cooking chips. Saturday was sausage and mash. When we were young, we always ate our pudding first, using the same plate for our meat course. Mother used to say that nine dinner-plates were quite enough to wash up every day. That was when the family was on its own. When we had company, we reverted to the correct way.

Mother made many kinds of delicious puddings. Dropped batter was a great favourite. It sounds funny 'dropped batter' – it was simply batter with any kind of fruit dropped in it, then cooked in the usual way. Treacle or jam sponge, spotted dick and bread and butter puddings were much enjoyed but the fruit pies, which we had all the year round because mother bottled every kind of fruit, were the best of all. I often heard mother say: "We are not rich but my family has always been well-fed and clothed."

Which reminds me of my Aunt Sarah, who used to ask us kids in turn for Sunday dinner. She was a good cook, but what fascinated us was her husband, Uncle Harry, when he carved the joint. He would give us a delightful grin and ask: "Would you like a slice of dead pig?" or dead cow, or dead sheep (which he pronounced "ship"). After carving each slice, he would lick the carving knife and both sides from handle to point. How he managed to do this without cutting his tongue, I cannot think.

After Sunday dinner, weather permitting, we kids would be expected to go for long walks before attending Sunday school, to give father a bit of peace and quiet.

Washing in my mother's day was a very hard task, especially with such a large family. Our wash-house was about ten yards away from our kitchen door and there my mother had to fill a copper with water from the pump in the kitchen, which was fed from a cistern filled with rainwater from the house roof. In summer this cistern ran dry and very hard water from the well had to be used. She said it was so hard one could not get a decent lather. This water also furred up our copper kettles with a kind of beige-coloured slate. They became so heavy and held so little water, they had to be sent away to be professionally defurred.

Mother began by sorting the clothes, first the tablecloths, sheets, pillowcases and tea towels, then the girls' white Sunday dresses and the boys' white shirts, then the very pale colours. The clothes were swished around with a dolly peg in a dolly tub half-filled with hot water from the copper, to which a cupful of Hudson's washing powder was added. Hudson's was the very first washing-powder that came on the market, but we did have a special kind of soap called Preservene which was highly regarded. The clothes were then boiled in soapy water in the copper for around fifteen minutes, taken out and rinsed in another dolly tub of clean water, then rinsed again in water that had a bit of Reckitt's Blue in it, and lastly put into starched water and hung out to dry. This was time-consuming as well as terribly hard work, and after I was born mother could not possibly manage washdays alone.

Sadly, a few days after I was born, my mother's favourite brother died suddenly of pneumonia. Mother could not go to see him while he was ill, and she was still confined on the funeral day. This, I was told, upset her terribly. Afterwards his widow, our favourite Auntie Lottie, came to see mother and there and then it was decided that for a time she would come to help us several days a week. When we were older, she told us children that we had saved her reason after the loss of her beloved husband only two years after their marriage. Aunt Lottie came on Mondays and Tuesdays to help with the washing, for the wash was too large to be done in one day. She came to help clean the bedrooms on Thursdays and again on Saturdays to clean the downstairs rooms. Mother used to talk of being clean for Sunday when no extra cleaning was allowed.

Bathing was an organized operation and was quite a comfortable experience before a good kitchen fire. As all seven children were living at home, we had one bath night, always on a Saturday.

Mother started with the baby, then John and so on until all the children were bathed. She used to take out a ladle or two full of water after each bath and added more hot water before the next child got in. When it came to the older children's turns, the whole bath was emptied and a fresh start was made with all clean water. Over the fire was a rack where the towels and our clean clothes were being kept beautifully warm and ready to wear.

When bathing as a child, I suffered from a great weakness. Though mother always made sure we kids all went out to the closet before bathing, the minute my body touched the water, I badly needed to wee. Quite often I did this surreptitiously in the bath, but mother was aware of this weakness and kept a close eye and ear on me. Suddenly she would say: "Nellie, what are you doing?" I would just have to tell her the truth. Then there would be much displeasure all round while the bath was emptied and a fresh start was made.

As we got older, bathing one after the other like this became more difficult, as we needed more privacy and liked more than one bath a week, so we did the same as our parents: prepared the kitchen ourselves and bathed behind locked doors and drawn blinds.

We were strictly brought up as regards Sundays. On that day we did not get up until eight o'clock, then we were dressed in our best clothes and, after a special breakfast, were sent off to Sunday school, after which we attended the morning service in St Mary's Church. On arriving home, we sat down to that delicious roast beef dinner. In the afternoon we went to Sunday school again and after tea to the evening service, winter nights excepted.

Sunday evenings we had a special supper. After bread and cheese, with no butter on the bread, we had a choice of treacle tart or egg custard. One Sunday evening we youngsters got the giggles. Mother asked us several times to quieten down but we only became worse, so then we were threatened with no treacle tart or egg custard. Still we could not stop, so mother took up the cane she rarely used, tapped us on our bottoms and sent us to bed. It was some time before we all calmed down and realized that we were now supper-less and, what was worse, treacle tart-less and egg custard-less.

We were not allowed to read newspapers on Sunday in case our Grandma Wootton came to see us. If she caught us reading newspapers or non-religious books on Sunday, we were in deep trouble with her. We loved and respected her so much that this telling-off made a great impression on us. In spite of this we managed on summer days to read "this rubbish", as she called it, in the orchard and on other days in the outbuildings where we played.

Sometimes on winter nights our Auntie Lottie would come and stay with us children while our parents went to church. We loved these nights with our favourite auntie who entertained us with stories of her childhood. One evening she told us that the brooch she was wearing would be for my sister Lottie; this was a gold one forming the word "Lottie". Auntie said that in her will I would receive her other gold brooch, the one with a little red stone. Childlike, I had no idea what a will was and wanted the brooch there and then. Wills were explained but I grew more and more upset at not having the brooch immediately. To my everlasting regret, I did a shameful thing: I cut right through the ribbon on my auntie's best hat, under the bow, so she wouldn't see it, but, of course, when she put the hat on, the whole ribbon fell off. She knew instantly who the culprit was and why it had been done. She looked so sad and upset that I should do such a thing against her and in all my life I never felt so mean. The mental agony I suffered for a long time taught me never to be such a little bitch again.

A conversation between my mother and Auntie Lottie is one of my earliest memories. Auntie Lottie said to mother: "I received a pot of paste from a friend and I had to tell her I liked it before she would tell me what it was made of. Do you know, Mary, the paste was delicious, but you would never in a lifetime guess what it was made from. It was mouse paste." Now I was very curious to know just what mouse paste tasted like, so I went out to one of our buildings where we often found dead mice. I found one that did not look too old and I skinned it, never thinking of the insides. I put it in an old rusty blacklead tin, then surreptitiously crept into the kitchen, opened the oven door and popped in the mouse. Mother called from our living room: "What are you doing near that stove, Nell?" I made an excuse that was accepted and, after a short wait, I opened the oven door, but the poor old mouse looked exactly as it did when I had put it in the oven: a revolting mess. The oven was full of sticks drying in readiness for lighting the next morning's fire. My mother, now feeling suspicious, came out to see what I was about, but by that time I had quickly snatched the mouse and tin out of the oven, had run outside and was bravely tasting the mouse. Horrible, horrible! Mother never knew just what I was doing that day. Very few of my friends believe this story, saying I must have heard something that sounded like mouse paste. Nevertheless I did skin, cook and taste the dead mouse.

One of the things we kids got up to when mother was out was to make a paste to spread on our bread and butter. We would half fill a cup with sugar and cocoa, then carefully mix it with milk to just the right consistency to spread it on our bread without it running off.

Lottie was seldom in hot water, but her liking for meat once got us both into trouble. When mother made pork pies, Lottie and I used to change her crust for my meat. Mother caught us out several times, warning us not to do this, as Lottie was getting all the protein and I all the starch. We could not understand this jargon and still changed the food under the table. At last mother gave us an ultimatum: dry toast and no pie if this happened again. It did, of course, and we suffered accordingly, for we ate dry toast while watching the rest of the family eating mother's delicious porkpie. Needless to say, we never exchanged the crust and the meat ever again.

4 GROWING UP

When we were small children, the older ones had to look after the younger ones. An amusing example was when my brother Warner took my sister to Sunday school. On arrival Florrie wanted to wee and Warner could not manage to remove her knickers. The vicar was passing by, so Warner said: "Our Flo wants to pee, vicar, and I can't get her knickers down. Can you?" This story was recounted by a lady Sunday-school teacher and when asked "What did the vicar say?", the answer was "Oh! he said: 'Tut, tut.'" Mr Green, our vicar, was a stern disciplinarian. We children were frightened to death of him. Once at Sunday school I had a new hat which I was very proud of. I expect I was prinking and preening instead of singing the hymn. Suddenly my head was banged by a heavy hymn book. I was very upset, but more for the damage to my hat than to my hurt head.

It was not very often that we had new clothes. Florrie, being the eldest, was the fortunate one, as she seemed to have nearly all the new ones. Material was made to last. Lottie had to wear Florrie's outgrown garments, then they were handed down to me. However, I was such a tear-away, they were too worn out to be handed down to Edna May, so she had a fair share of new ones. Once a year mother used to take us to Loughborough, usually in the autumn, to buy us our winter outfits. This was a terrific adventure. First, we had to be ready by eight o'clock to catch the ride to Loughborough in the carrier's cart. This was constructed like the old road caravans with small windows that one had to stand on the seats to look through. Mr Arnold, who owned and drove this horse-drawn van, went round the villages on the way ringing a bell, and people came out with a basket and a written list of articles for him to bring back for them, so the five-mile journey took over two hours. The same thing happened on the return journey as the baskets and parcels were delivered, and we would arrive home in the evening around six. One year, mother said we were all to have new coats and I was excited beyond belief. Mother dressed us girls as much alike as possible and this time she had decided saxe blue was the colour she would like.

When we arrived at the coat shop, mother told the assistant she wanted a saxe blue coat for all four girls. This was rather a tall order and it was not forthcoming. Florrie, Lottie and Edna May were well set up with coats alike, but there was not one to fit me. Their coats cost 15/6d each and I was upset not to have one like the others. The lady brought a dark blue coat, costing 14/6d, but mother decided the quality was poor. Next came a beautiful astrakhan russet-coloured coat, which I loved on sight and I was dying to try it on. It fitted perfectly with enough room for a year's growth. Mother liked it but the price was staggering: 17/6d. "Far too much for a child's coat," she said.

The suspense was hurting badly and must have shown in my face. I could only mutter: "I don't remember ever having a brand-new coat." Mother started to make excuses why I should have this expensive coat: "Nell is quite right. She always has to wear hand-me-downs. When she outgrows it, Edna May will look very nice in it." I had my new coat, my russet brown astrakhan coat, along with a new saxe blue hat exactly like those of my three sisters. Tired and excited, we made our way to the Green Man public house, where Mr Arnold put up his horse and van.

The following Sunday mother dressed us all in our new hats and coats to go to Sunday school. To me she said: "Nell, you must be especially careful wearing such an expensive coat." The night before, snow had fallen, leaving the dirt roads like a quagmire. We carefully picked our way, but when we reached a farm gateway where cows which had just been let out had left their usual mess, I immediately tried to jump over it, but unluckily I fell into quite the worst of it. My sisters and I were petrified. What would mother say? First time out and for this to happen. I turned back home, disconsolate beyond all bearing. Mother gave one look at my cow-dirty, wet, beautiful new coat. She helped me out of it, put me into my very old coat and sent me back to Sunday school. I was not smacked, as mother was so understanding. She immediately washed the affected part, but always a slight stain remained.

Our infants' school was one huge room divided by a screen which was raised up to the ceiling when the room was used for parties or wedding receptions. There was a huge open fire at each end. Miss Smith taught the babies and Miss Parish the second class. They had a system that the first child in class sat nearest the fire and so on, until the poorest scholar who sat furthest away had to wear her outdoor coat in extreme weathers, but if a child brought a letter from a parent which stated that the child was unwell, then she or he would be allowed a special place near teacher and very close to the fire. When we reached the third class, we were sent to the National School that had three rooms, two of which were heated by the same method. The largest room had a huge stove in the middle. The kids loved to congregate around it when the weather was unfit for us to go out to play.

I had a favourite teacher who used to bring her three-year-old niece, Kathleen, to school and then allow one of the older girls to take her the three hundred yards back home. I loved this little girl and always asked for the privilege of taking her home but this was refused for a long time. My persistence paid off, for eventually teacher said I could be the one that day. After being told that I must be careful and that I was like a cat on hot bricks, I set off hand in hand with the little niece, delivering her home safely to her waiting mum. The next Saturday, dressed in my oldest clothes, I made my way to see if I could play with Kathleen. Her grandma was cleaning shoes on a stone slab outside the kitchen door. As I walked up the path, she asked me what I wanted and I asked: "May I play with Kathleen?" "No, you cannot. Run along, little girl." Neither of us realized she was shooing away the little girl who one day would marry her beloved grandson and become mistress of the farmhouse she was sending me away from. In spite of this, my friendship with Kathleen lasted a lifetime, she became my sister-in-law and my best friend, and we have been through sad and happy times together.

Sometimes, when we came out of school, the rag and bone man would be waiting outside in the street and he would tell us children to ask our parents to send all their rags, bones and rabbit skins back to school with us. He would pay us either a few coppers or a couple of goldfish. If we wanted a fish, we had to take a jam jar full of water, but I always chose the money because everyone's goldfish seemed to die within a few days.

One day I was smacked at school and went home crying. Father asked me why I was slapped and I answered: "For nothing." "Oh no!" said father, Miss Smith doesn't smack children for nothing." At last he got the truth out of me. I had been naughty, so father smacked me, saying: "Don't come home crying again that the teacher has hit you for nothing." I never did: after being chastised twice, I learned my lesson.

During my childhood I had two horrible recurring dreams which I have never forgotten. One was, as I was lying in bed, the door opened and I saw a little man walk up to my bed. His face was a cabbage, his body a long sort of cabbage with green spindly arms and legs, but as he was going to touch me, I always woke up screaming. The other was, I followed my father on to the roof of a Wymeswold three-storey house, but I always woke up falling off.

One day a friend of mine named Gertie Walker asked me to tea. Mother washed me and dressed me with a white pinny made of broderie anglaise. When we arrived at her house, her mother asked me: "Why are you wearing your best pinnie, Nellie?" Then she said: "Sit on the sofa until we have finished our tea, then Gertie can come out to play with you." Gertie hadn't the pluck to tell her mother she had asked me for tea, and neither had I, but my mother was highly amused when I went home hungry as a hunter and she had to prepare another tea, after she had already cleared the family's tea things away.

My brother Warner, whom I adored, suffered with winter chilblains which itched dreadfully when he became warm in bed, so he asked me if I would get into his bed and scratch these tiresome big toes. This I did, but then he used to challenge me to see how many scratches I could do in one evening. The challenge became higher and higher, reaching five hundred scratches. Much as I loved him, I got tired of this job, but he always managed to inveigle one of the younger kids to do this for him, until my mother stopped it, saying we were getting too old to be in bed with our brother. Then my young brothers were asked to do the scratching.

When I was in any way troubled, I had a secret hideaway where I could ponder until I felt better. It was an old willow tree that was completely hollow, with an opening in the trunk just wide enough for a small child to creep into. It stood at the side of a brook in my grandfather Wootton's field. I spent many hours inside that old tree. Sadly it is no more, as houses have been built in that field now.

During the first World War some of the Wymeswold farmers were sent German prisoners to work on their farms. A friend of my father's, John Smith, who later became my father-in-law, was sent one of these men. The prisoner slept in their barn and was supposed to eat only the ration stipulated by the Ministry. Mr Smith was lucky in having a fine man working for him and was sorry to see him work so hard on such a meagre ration, so he took him a nice hot dinner into the barn whenever they had one themselves, although he would have been in trouble with the Ministry, had they known about it.

There lived a man in our village called Mr Dykes, who for years walked the five miles to his work and back again. When he retired, he became one of our roadmen. In my young days these roadmen kept our village nice and tidy. This was extremely hard work with our dirt roads, but they kept the pathways clean and tidy and free from weeds. In winter, after snow fell, they would be clearing the paths with huge scrapers even before we children went to school. Nowadays even the town pathways are not cleared the way ours were in my youth. Rates in those days were minimal, an average of three to four pounds per year for a three-bedroomed house.

When I was around eleven years old, my grandfather Wootton asked me if I would collect the rents from the dozen or so cottages that he owned and let to families of various sizes. The rent for most of these cottages was 1/6d per week, but for two of them it was only 1/3d per week. I think grandfather sent me because he had become tired of the tenants wanting their cottages modernized but refusing to pay a higher rent. Grandfather told them he could not possibly spend a lot of money on the cottages without raising the rent considerably. Most of these cottages had one large living-room, a small kitchen and two medium-sized bedrooms. When grandfather died, the cottages were sold and the tenants were shocked at the many rent increases they suffered, but few improvements were made until after the Second World War. When each cottage became vacant, the new owners modernized them and then they were rented for many pounds per week. An old village character lived in one of the cottages and he used to get very drunk. I was told by grandfather that if this man was drunk, I was to leave the cottage straightaway, as he had been known to turn nasty when under the influence. I was always frightened when I came to this house and, if he was drunk, I ran away. Sometimes he would refuse to pay the rent but he was never nasty to me. Grandfather then had to visit him to see what he could do to make him pay up. All the tenants had little red books which I had to sign when I received the rent. Grandfather built two new large cottages which he called Jubilee Cottages. These had two large front rooms, a large kitchen and a pantry that was down some brick steps. Pantries were always built below ground level to keep the food cool. Nowadays refrigerators have done away with the need for this kind of pantry and present-day owners are having them filled in up to ground level.

During my early childhood there were no house or public telephones, just one at the Post Office which was used by all the village in case of emergency. I myself was phone shy and never spoke over the phone until I was over twenty years old. I liked letter writing and it only cost one penny to post a letter and a halfpenny for a postcard. The postman brought the post to Wymeswold from

Loughborough on his bicycle in a huge carrier on the front. In all those years none of the postmen was ever molested. One postman named Taylor cycled for years bringing the letters to the village, winter and summer alike, in all weathers.

We also had a man whose job it was to light the oil street-lamps every night in winter, but this was stopped during the First World War and never started again. It was not until 1933 that we had street lighting again when electric power was brought to our village. What a difference electricity made to these villages, with the lighting installed in almost every house. Only the rich installed the power, and it was many years before everyone gave up their flat irons for an electric one. Electric toasters, vacuum cleaners, fires, kettles and cookers were gradually purchased but not until after the Second World War did electric washing-machines find their way into the ordinary home.

5   ACCIDENTS AND ILLNESSES

Mother had her fair share of children's accidents and illnesses to cope with. The first accident I remember happened to me when I was six years old. I was racing up the garden path past our outdoor pump, just as my brother Warner was raising the pump handle sharply to get a drink of water. The handle hit me with great force under the chin, making me bite halfway through my tongue. The bleeding was so bad that mother could not ascertain where it was coming from. Warner was so upset he couldn't tell her what had happened, so she picked me up in her arms and raced through the village streets to the resident doctor's house. Fortunately he was at home, found the trouble quickly and immediately stitched the tongue in place again. Such was the calibre of most country doctors in those days. We had no cars in which to rush such cases five miles to our nearest hospital. A doctor had to do the job himself or allow a patient to bleed to death. The loss of blood was so great, it necessitated five weeks in bed. I could not speak at all, living only on slops. In my late sixties my tongue developed a varicose vein on the underside and my present-day doctor said the accident had weakened the vein which might not have been perfectly mended.

My parents always came into our bedroom before they retired, to see if we were alright and to tuck us up. One night, as they were leaving, wrongly assuming I was asleep, father whispered to mother: "Mary, that child will never speak again." I worried greatly about this, especially as I was the chatterbox of the family. After four weeks of not being able to move my tongue, I felt the paralysis gradually leaving it, so I started trying to articulate. It was terribly hard work and painful, my tongue felt like a piece of wood, but I secretly persevered. After about a week I was talking like Donald Duck, which caused a lot of laughter from my brothers and sisters, but I didn't mind one little bit because I was making progress in moving my stiff tongue. One day Grandma Wootton brought me a dinner of minced chicken, greens and mashed potatoes with lashings of gravy. It was surely the nicest meal I had ever tasted, not having had a proper meal for over five weeks. After my recovery father used to say: "Nell has certainly made up for lost time. Her tongue never stops."

The next bad accident happened to my sister Lottie. She was always the delicate one of the family and she lost a lot of schooling because of her weak chest. She usually sat watching the rest of us romping around. One day she was sitting on the handle of the chaff-cutter, a machine used for cutting hay and straw into chaff, which was mixed with sliced mangolds and turnips as food for our horses. After a while she started swinging backwards and forwards, forgetting we had been told repeatedly never to sit on this machine handle. Then she absent-mindedly put her arm under the knife, which cut a great gash in her wrist, only just missing the artery. Lottie had another bad accident when we were playing on top of a dray which had been backed up to a heap of lime used in the building trade. Lottie fell off the back of the dray, face down in the lime. The lime filled her eyes, blinding her for a long time and weakening her eyes permanently.

Among the various illnesses we children suffered, one of the two most serious was scarlet fever, a notifiable disease. This necessitated six weeks' isolation and, with six children contracting the illness in one family, from beginning to end it was more than eight weeks. We were all put into one room with a fireplace, for we had no other form of heating, no gas or electricity. Mother had to carry the fuel to heat the room from up the yard which was quite eighty or more yards from the house. We were halfway through our isolation when mother became ill. She told the doctor she thought she, too, had caught the scarlet fever and, though he looked at her chest and said "Rubbish", she got worse and eventually her whole body peeled just like the rest of us. Mother's illness gave rise to great difficulties and father had to isolate himself from his family, for he could not risk getting the disease because of his building commitments. Grandma Wootton, who fortunately lived only a street away, was wonderful at this dreadful time: she not only looked after father, she left hot dinners at the door and fetched sticks and coal for the fires. Nowadays scarlet fever is not the dreaded disease it was many years ago.

We had all or most of the children's illnesses, like mumps, measles, whooping-cough and chicken-pox, but the other serious disease, perhaps the worst of them all, was diphtheria. All except Florrie, who was living with a friend, fell with this disease, even little Bill, the three-month-old baby. Mother called the doctor, who immediately diagnosed diphtheria and sent for the serum to inject us. Mother called out to the neighbours living on each side of us to keep their children away from our house because of this illness. Young John Brain, living on our left side, never came near our place to our knowledge but, sadly, he caught diphtheria and died. Then there was little May Elliott, living opposite, who stole out of her house while her mother was cheese making, climbed two high gates and came into our kitchen. There she found a bowl of gruel baby Billie had refused and started eating it with the same spoon used by my brother. Mother, who took her home, advised her mother to call the doctor. May's mother was a very busy woman and my mother had so much on her mind with six of her own children who might well die. Unfortunately their prayers were not answered and little May caught the disease and died an agonizing death. We children were too ill to realize all this until later and were shocked when we learned of the deaths of our little playmates. I was thirteen when we contracted diphtheria. I loved our little baby like he was my own and nursed him all day and every day. He slept in my arms at night and the only times he left me was when mother suckled him. Lottie was very ill indeed, but she and the rest of us all recovered.

Before having diphtheria, I was a fair soprano singer and a member of the junior church choir. When I attended my first practice after I was better, I realized I could not reach any higher than C, whereas I had been able to reach F and G quite easily. The choir-mistress spoke to me quite sharply and asked: "Nellie, why do you stop singing your high notes?" When I told her I could not reach them now, she said: "Right, we'll see how low you can get." Surprisingly, I sang right down to G and later on lower still. I was exceedingly proud to be the only child contralto in the church choir, afterwards singing solos, duets and quartets in the senior choir. As a family we had a quartet on our own. Father was a good singer, taking the tenor parts. Brother Warner sang bass, Florrie had a good soprano voice and I filled in with the contralto. Sometimes we were asked to sing in the chapel at Rempstone. On Sunday evenings many of our friends would gather round our piano, where we enjoyed a good old sing-song. Those were such happy times.

While we were in quarantine with two illnesses, mother bought a lot of dishcloth cotton and even my eldest brother learned to knit. We knitted scores of dishcloths which were left in the room to be fumigated along with everything else. Before fumigation all the wallpaper and ceiling paper had to be stripped, so towards the end of our confinement mother wisely allowed us to strip every piece off and gradually burn it. We enjoyed ourselves writing and drawing on the bare walls.

Father was always the one who chose the new wallpapers and in this case he chose a beautiful paper that had baskets of roses, pink and dark red ones. The doors and windows were painted white. We had new white lace curtains and even a fawn fitted carpet with a flower design, the only fitted carpet in the house. We four girls and our parents were exceedingly proud of this bedroom. We were made to keep it tidy ourselves. We each had our own drawer and vied with each other to see whose drawer could be kept the tidiest.

The time came when we all had colds. We had no tissues in those days, so mother used to save and wash all the old white materials such as sheets and pillowcases and tablecloths which were torn up into size-able squares and given to us when all the hankies were used up. Lottie had a very runny nose, so mother gave her an extra large piece of sheeting. One morning Florrie teased her unmercifully while we were dressing. Lottie had a quiet nature and hardly ever retaliated despite her sister's teasing, but on this particular morning she quietly dipped her sheeting into the 'gusunder' and shied the urine-saturated cloth straight at the teasing Florrie. She dodged the wet cloth which hit our beautiful red and pink rose wallpaper.' We watched in horror at the red stain running to the bottom of the wall down the skirting board, finishing up on our new fawn carpet. Mother called us several times to make haste as breakfast was ready, but we dared not go downstairs. Eventually mother realized something was wrong and came to fetch us down. The guilty look on all our faces told her we had done something bad. She enquired what the matter was. We all remained speechless but our eyes kept straying to the messed up wall. She gave one look and said: "I don't know what your father will say, but you will all be late for school, if you don't come downstairs and have your breakfast." My father was told what Lottie had done and, after looking at it, said: "I am not going to smack you all. Your punishment will be looking at this unsightly mess, as I will not have a new piece of paper put on." He was quite right: we all suffered greatly at seeing our bedroom spoiled. We other girls were under no illusions as regards our punishment: father never smacked Lottie because of her delicate state of health but, had it been one of us other three, we would all have had our bottoms well and truly smacked.

One thing mother insisted upon was our Saturday morning dose of one teaspoonful of treacle and brimstone before breakfast. Mother said this was to keep us healthy and to clear our blood. Whether it did or not I do not know, but mother had seven children and all are alive at the present time, the oldest having just turned eighty and the youngest being a sixty-year-old, which must be a good record.

A terrible thing happened to me when I was seven years old, for I ate some old kidney bean seeds and nearly poisoned myself. I was so ill, mother thought I would die. I always seemed to be in trouble, for it came to me again one summer a few years later. I took Mrs Roe's baby for an outing in his pram. Mrs Roe, a busy farmer's wife, was no doubt pleased for her baby to be out in his pram, but she thought I looked a bit small for the job. She asked me how old I was and, after great hesitation, allowed me to take baby Roe out most evenings and paid me twopence a week. Everything went well till I met a friend who was older than I and was also pushing a pram. We had an argument about who had the prettiest baby and, although I knew full well that my friend had, I would not concede this, so she challenged me to a pram race. We must have been mad, for this race took place down the steepest hill leading from our village. The prams were keeping quite level when we heard a horse and cart coming round the bend at the bottom of the hill. My friend pulled up safely, but I was not so lucky and my pram turned over, tipping out my six-month-old baby. I picked him up, none the worse for his tumble, but my conscience would not allow me to keep quiet about the affair. I took the baby home and confessed to his mother just what I had done. She was very upset and would not let me take out the baby again. I pleaded with Mrs Roe but she was firm and did not let me take him out again for a long time. Really, I loved babies and was very good with them. I was allowed to nurse him and play with him at his home, which kept him good and was a help to his mother. Eventually I was forgiven and trusted once again and I never did anything so silly again.

6 GAMES AND ESCAPADES

When we were young, we certainly had to create our own amusements. In summer the game of whip and top was very popular with both boys and girls like myself. We would challenge each other to see who could keep their top spinning the longest time. The same boy nearly always won. He had a special whip and top skill that nobody else had. I think today he would be called a whip-and-top child prodigy. Marbles were played with one large glass marble each, called a taw. A coin would be spun to see who would start the play, then one would roll his marble a reasonable distance away and the other would try to hit it. If a marble was hit, it was lost and the next player would take his turn. Sometimes we made bets on how many marbles one should forfeit if one lost. I played this game with my brother Warner many times. With a girl I knew I used to play a game called snobs. We used to sit on some doorsteps belonging to my friend's neighbour, who was very proud of them. She always kept them in immaculate condition and hated to see children playing on them. She asked us several times to keep off her steps, but we didn't until one day, halfway through our game, we heard her bedroom window open. To our horror, as we looked up, she emptied her chamber pot all over us. Needless to say, after that we never played snobs on that step again. Hopscotch and skipping were much enjoyed by the girls and many hours were spent playing battledore and shuttlecock.

In winter we played ticky on our journeys to school and this lively game helped to keep us warm. When we had snow and frost, it would be snowballing time and making slides down Church Street, which had just the right incline for a long slide. We would take a lot of time making a smooth slide the whole length of this street, continuing it round the corner on to the main street, called Far Street. This slide was by far the most thrilling of our winter games. Unfortunately the village policeman would often cover the slide with ashes while we were in school. We had to be content with smaller slides which we were allowed to keep in our school playground. Owing to present day traffic, children cannot play these street games.

The children in our family were especially lucky to live in a builder's yard. We used to borrow one of the carpenter's trestles, struggle with one of the heavy planks used in the scaffolding and place it over the trestle. Lo and behold, we would have a perfect see-saw, strong enough to carry half a dozen children each side. We played see-saw for hours and hours. The only danger was to the fingers if we allowed them to get trapped between the plank and the trestle. Father's strong ropes also came in handy when we played swinging from the apple trees. Warner would climb the tree and secure the rope, then he would make a seat from wood in the yard and great competition took place to see who could swing the highest. Sometimes two would swing together, one of the smaller children sitting and an older child standing with feet astride the child on the seat.

Two empty tins were used in another enjoyable game. A large hole was made in the top of each tin and a piece of binder string was pulled through. A double knot was used to keep in the string and then, with a foot on each tin and holding the string in each hand, we would try to master the art of walking on tins. We became quite good at this game and enjoyed organizing races for the various age groups. Tins had another use when they were filled with small stones to make rattles for babies. We also had fun making a noise running around with tins on strings, dragging them along the ground with stones inside them. We had no expensive toys, only this kind of home-made ones.

A story was told to me about a snowballing escapade in which several Wymeswold boys took part. One of the boys, called Willie Taylor, made a big snowball around a stone which he threw straight through a public house window. All the other boys ran away but Willie stood his ground. The publican came out terribly angry, shouting: "Which way have the little buggers gone?" Quite calmly Willie pointed in the opposite direction, waited for the irate

publican to return and asked him if he had caught them. The publican replied breathlessly: "No, I didn't. I missed the little blighters."

This same Willie used to be Wymeswold's ace of practical jokers. One could fill a book with Willie's jokes. How he thought them up, one cannot comprehend. The following are a few of the pranks he played on his friends. Once he collected a group of people in a public house, told them he had a new wonder camera and asked them to stand in a group. Putting them in position with great to-do, he said: "Wait a minute. We must have a vase of flowers on this table." After placing the flowers, he said: "Smile, please." Willie told them all to meet again the following Saturday when he would bring with him the proofs for them all to see. Everyone arrived on the Saturday, eagerly looking forward to seeing just what sort of pictures this long, thin, new sort of camera would take, but with a sorrowful face Willie told them the photographs had not turned out, so he went through the whole procedure again. When everyone came the next Saturday, Willie showed the people his new camera, which was one of the first new Biro pens and said: "Have you ever been had?"

This was taken in good part, unlike his next trick in a Wymeswold public house. He was sitting against the publican's son when he whispered to him: "Can you smell something, Bill?" The answer was: "No, why? Can you?" "Yes, I can," said Willie, holding his nose while looking around on the floor for the cause. "Dear, dear:" says Willie, "there is something under my chair needs clearing away." "Shut up, for God's sake!" says Bill. "Don't let my mother know about this mess or she'll go mad." Bill quietly got up and fetched a dustpan with a few ashes on it and surreptitiously gathered the offending dog dirt on to it. He took it outside, followed by Willie Taylor who rescued the plastic dog dirt in readiness for another prank in another pub. His friend Bill was furious and called him unrepeatable names.

Another of his pranks was played on one of his friends who was a policeman. Willie pinned a toilet roll to the back of his uniform coat and the policeman proceeded to walk through the Loughbor-ough market-place with an ever-lengthening trail of toilet paper. Willie is now retired and over eighty years old. He recently met his policeman friend who reminded him about this particular prank. Willie didn't always get away with these tricks. Sometimes they boomeranged, then Willie was not too pleased.

Lottie and I once had a bird's-eye view of two neighbours, both over eighty years old, quarrelling about the boundary between their gardens which were divided by a foot and a half grass path. Mr Smith accused Mr Maltby of taking a bit more of his path every time he dug his garden. This enraged Mr Smith until he could contain his anger no longer and, after shouting at each other for around ten minutes, the two men began to fight. Poor Mr Smith got the worst of it, because Mr Maltby kept grabbing his long beard and swinging him round and round. Mr Smith conceded defeat in the fight but not about the encroachment on his garden.

We kids used to watch the Brickhill engine which puffed up our yard to empty the bricks. These steam engines were used before petrol engines took over. They were able to carry huge loads but were much slower than the modern lorries. They came to our village only occasionally. The horses were frightened to death of them. Sometimes a horse would not face up to them: it would stop, turn around and race away in the opposite direction. Sometimes the men who brought father's building materials would swear like troopers and we kids would use the same language to each other, but woe betide us if mother ever heard us. She would say to us: "Children, there are enough words in the English dictionary to express oneself without using swear words."

Christmas at home was a very happy time, for mother would go to a lot of trouble to make it so. We would hang up one of father's stockings made from a mixture of black and dark-red wool which came up over the knee; these were the biggest stockings we could find. We would pin a garter on to the top of the stocking, then pass it over the brass knob on our bed, always at the bottom end. There was great excitement in the morning when we would find an

orange, an apple, a white sugar mouse with a pink nose and tail, some chocolates and sweets, a Christmas stocking in pink and white gauze filled with knick-knacks and sweets, and perhaps one large present. We never had a Christmas tree but we had a holly bush hanging from a hook in the ceiling with tinsel and coloured baubles shining all around it and we would spin this creation round and round. After dinner we all looked forward to the last and best present of all which was given to us by Miss Simpson who kept the shop in our street. Father was in charge of these presents and would tease us unmercifully. When we asked for the gifts, he would say: "Let your dinner go down first." Then it would be: "Wait till I have smoked my cigar." Next it would be: "Wait till your mother comes in." Any excuse to keep us in suspense. Another ruse was when he said: "Would you like a puff of my cigar?" We nearly all had one puff, which was quite enough to make us choke and cough for a long time. We were given an orange each and even that had to be used to tease us. Father would pretend to give us the orange, then throw it up into the air time and time again. Eventually we were given the orange and the big present from Miss Simpson. Mother would say to father that he would spoil his children's tempers with his teasing.

During the Christmas festivities mother would give us a slap-up party at home, inviting many of our friends. She said we were a party every day, there being nine of us in our family, and she could not give us birthday parties as they came far too often. Mother was marvellous at arranging games for young people. Postman's knock was a great favourite. Then we used to play fives and sevens or fizz-buzz. This game was played with everyone sitting in a circle and each counting in turn. The first person started with one, the second with two, the third three and the fourth four, but the fifth had to say fizz and thereafter any number divisible by five was fizz. When it came to seven, the person would say buzz and every number divisible by seven was buzz. When one came to fifty-one, that was fizz-one, fifty-five was fizz-fizz, fifty-six was fizz-buzz, as was fifty-seven. Seventy-one was buzz-one and seventy-seven buzz-buzz, and so the game progressed. When one got it wrong, one was out of the game. It was a marvellous test of mental arithmetic and could be quite exciting, for often, when it came to the last two or three players, the numbers had reached well over a hundred.

During our minor illnesses which kept us away from school, and during winter nights in the warm glow of the oil lamps, mother would teach us card games, draughts and Halma. I generally beat Lottie at these games and mother, who always felt sympathy with the loser, would peer over our shoulders and give a little help to Lottie, enabling her to win the game. Lottie liked snakes and ladders more than games like whist and lexicon. We all loved the game of snap at which I considered myself the champion, but Edna used to say: "No, our Nell, you pick up the cards before anyone else has a chance, whether you called first or not."

As I grew older, I became an avid reader of any books I could lay my hands on. I remember reading a story of a little dark-haired girl around seven years of age who was always getting into trouble. As the story continued, I kept thinking: "That girl is just like me: little, dark-haired and always in trouble." Further in the story someone told the little girl she was an adopted child and was not really one of the family. The sorrow of this little girl affected me so deeply, I began to worry in case I was adopted, too. Mother noticed my unusual downcast behaviour and eventually asked me what was the matter. I then blurted out: "Am I your own child or am I adopted?" My mother's surprise was so great, I knew what her answer would be. She seemed nonplussed, saying; "Whatever put that idea into your head, child?" I told her about the story I had been reading and how I had brooded on the matter for weeks. She kissed me and told me to forget all about it.

From the age of around eight years, I loved making up stories "out of my head", as my sisters called it. As soon as we were settled in bed, they would say: "Tell us a story, our Nell." Our Nell did not need any persuading and I would go on and on to such an extent that father became alarmed at the amount of sleep we were losing. At last he gave us an ultimatum: I could tell stories until he rapped on the ceiling under our bedroom and then I was to stop and all of us were to go to sleep. The next night the rapping came loud and clear, so I said to my sisters; "Not one more word," and put my head under the bedclothes. They kept on pleading: "Please finish the story, our Nell," but our Nell said: "Not another word."

The girls got cross with me, talking louder and louder, until finally father came upstairs, turned the bedclothes down and my night-gown up and smacked my bottom thoroughly. My sisters never spoke a word in my defence, so I told them I would never forgive them for their disloyalty and would never, never tell them another story as long as I lived. I kept this vow for a few nights, but I suffered much more at not telling the stories than my sisters did at not hearing them. I was so happy to capitulate and get cracking on my imaginary people and animals once again.

Another thing I enjoyed doing, aided by my sister Florrie, was making rag dolls out of old black stockings, putting in their faces with coloured wool for eyes and nose and red wool for the lips. We would dress them in all kinds of paper dresses, coloured paper when available, and newspaper when we had nothing better. The old-fashioned pegs were useful, too. We would paint the top for the face and make them lovely full dresses. I never had a real doll until I was ten years old and Florrie started work. With some of her first earnings she bought me a doll, which I treasured, until one of my own children dropped it and broke the china face. To dress this doll, I coveted a half-yard of material I had seen in one of mother's bedroom drawers. I had asked her several times for this material but she had said: "No, it might come in useful sometime." This material was pale blue with a navy sprig. One day, when mother was out, I crept into her bedroom and took out the material, just to have a look at it. Then I was lost and, after a mental fight with myself, I took the material downstairs and cut out a dress for my doll. When mother saw the dressed doll, she was cross with me. I was not spanked, but she made me feel ashamed of myself. That was mother's way: she had only to look at us sometimes and we knew just what she was thinking.

I overheard her telling a friend about this episode and how she had chastised me, but the friend said: "Mary, you made a mistake in the first place by not giving Nellie the material. I think you were suppressing something in that child that needs encouraging." In later years when I was making dresses and coats for all my family, mother admitted she had been wrong.

7 ENTERTAINMENT

We children all attended the same Church of England school, run by the vicar with the help of prominent village gentlemen who were the school trustees. The church and school were the main centres of village life. Occasionally a missionary would come to our village to give services in the church. These services were well attended, partly because we were shown slides of other parts of the world which the missionary had visited. This was the knowledge we craved, not being able to learn of the outside world as present-day children can.

From my earliest days I remember Sunday school parties where we enjoyed a delicious tea. All the children took their own china and cutlery, which we were given strict instructions not to break or lose. After tea the room was cleared and we played all sorts of games. The one I liked best was called "Turn trench", played with a round wooden cheese board. A chosen child had to spin the cheese board while calling the name of someone who had to race out and catch it before it stopped spinning, If they failed to catch the board before it fell, they had to pay a forfeit. The forfeits given were the cause of terrific fun for everyone in the room. "Bite an inch off the poker" was hilarious, especially if the player did not know what to do – hold the poker one inch away from the mouth and then give a good bite in mid-air. Others were "Kissing the one you love best in the room" and "Dancing in the middle of the room". The forfeit of reciting a poem was found extremely difficult by some children. This may sound daft, but I have seen a whole roomful of people absolutely holding their sides with uncontrollable laughter.

In those days we made our own entertainments such as giving concerts. For these we had to practise regularly and this caused much fun, especially on the night before the first performance when we had the dress rehearsal. The children loved the singing and the acting.

I was thirteen years old before our village had a bus service; until then we never left the village except by horse and cart or on foot. Our Sunday school outing was looked forward to from one year to another. We were taken to Charnwood Forest in large waggons drawn by great shire horses lent by the farmers. These waggons held around twenty-five children and wooden rails were fixed to the sides to stop children falling out. We usually went to Woodhouse Eaves up Windmill Hill – the windmill is now burnt down – and sometimes up Beacon Hill. Mother told us a story of her youth up Beacon Hill. Her brother Bill was going steady with a Wymeswold girl called Lizzie. When the Wymeswold party reached the top, Lizzie went off with a boy from another party. Bill, who had carried Lizzie's basket of food to the top of the hill, raised it high in the air and threw it after them, shouting: "If he has you, he can have your basket."

We also had summer parties in local fields lent by farmers. There we would be entertained with all sorts of popular sports: three-legged races, tug-of-war, the potato race and, for the boys, high jumping. A friend and I loved practising the three-legged race and we often won in our age group. Garden parties were often held in the gardens of the richer residents. Mr Campion of Campion Cycles and his wife, who lived at Wymeswold Hall, gave freely of their time and money to help in the improvement of village life.

Christmas was a marvellous time for the village children. There was always a party in the Church schoolroom for all the village children, whether they were Wesleyan, Baptist or Church children. One party most remembered was given by a Dr Roberts who was leaving the village. Every child was given a really expensive present. Lottie was given a beautiful doll. How I envied her, for I yearned for a doll of my own. Lottie loved this doll, nursing it for hours on end when she was too poorly to go to school. She allowed me to nurse it only once in a while.

During our childhood years, when we were going to school concerts or parties, mother used to put our hair in rag curlers. We slept in these and kept them on during the day until half an hour before we went out. As a result, instead of four straight-haired daughters, she had four girls with the most lovely ringlets which only just lasted out the festivities. The usual way we styled our hair was to plait it before getting into bed and then comb it out before going to school. This left our hair in a wavy condition for a few hours only, for by dinner time our hair was once again "straight as a yard of pump water", as mother used to describe it.

The styles of our dresses were very different from the present way of dressing. The girls, next to the skin, wore long chemises reaching to the knees, made of thin cambric with lace round the neck in the summer and thick flannelette with feather stitching round the neck in the winter. We wore liberty bodices and dark-blue bloomers drawn over the top and a flannel underskirt for winter with a flannelette one on top as well. Next came our dress which reached to mid-calf and was made of thick woollen material. Over this we wore white pinnies or sprigged print ones. Special pinnies of broderie anglaise were worn on Sundays. Our dresses were also made of this lovely material with frills everywhere. The washing and ironing of these dresses was a lengthy business. Our boots were calf-high, with buttons all up the sides which were fastened with a button hook. Mother was often ironing our dresses on Sunday morning before we could go to church. The boys wore the same kind of clothing until they were four years old, but our last baby, born eighteen years after the first child, wore dresses only until he was two. Then the boys were put into baggy trousers reaching past their knees. Children's clothing is far more labour-saving and sensible nowadays.

After the First World War Mr and Mrs Campion, along with other willing helpers, started raising money to build a Memorial Hall in memory of our fallen boys. Eventually, after many garden fetes, concerts, dances, whist drives and sewing parties, the hall was built. I believe it took nearly a decade before everything was paid off in full. My father was one of the men who lent money, interest free, and these men were made the trustees of the hall. Certain rules were made for the use of the hall, including one that no intoxicating liquor be consumed on the premises. However, after many committee meetings and legal difficulties, this law was later altered so that the hall could be let for weddings and birthday parties. Another rule was that no lettings were to be made for entertainments on Sundays, so dances had to close sharp at midnight on Saturdays.

The tennis courts were laid in the grounds at the back of the hall; these were well used and popular. Matches were played against other village clubs. We travelled on bicycles or in the pony and float to reach these villages. Later on, the hall committee decided to take one of the tennis courts and lay a bowling green. The bowling club membership grew and grew but the tennis club membership went down and down. One could wait half the night before securing a game. Eventually the tennis club closed down. Wymeswold has never since enjoyed the pleasure of tennis and the court has now been converted into a small playground for infants.

Wymeswold has always had a cricket and football team. In father's time, when the cricket club played against the next village, the losing side had to pay for a dinner at the Three Crowns Inn in Wymeswold. The cricketers at the neighbouring village of Willoughby on the Wolds were fanatics and Wymeswold always had a tough job beating them. When we did win, our supporters went mad.

In my young day Wymeswold had a brass band. At every garden-party the band would march through the village playing the same old tunes, followed by nearly all the children in fancy dress. When everyone arrived at the grounds where the fete was held, the lady who opened the festivities would then judge the fancy dress competition, for which many prizes were given by people from the village.

One of the most popular entertainments was the annual flower-show and gymkhana that always took place on August Bank

Holiday Tuesday. There was great competition in the fruit and vegetable tent, along with a magnificent display of flowers and several handicraft stalls. Outside the main tent was a fair with all the usual side-shows. At five o'clock the sports and gymkhana started. Such was the enthusiasm for this event that, as soon as it was over, work was started to plan the next year's show. Unfortunately, after several bad, rainy days when the public did not attend, funds ran out and this splendid show was abandoned. I always feel sad when inclement weather, year after year, drains the resources for this type of entertainment.

Another event, held in November, was the annual visit of the fair to Loughborough for three days: Thursday, Friday and Saturday. We children never went to the fair until we were old enough to cycle or could take the bus which started to come through the village about 1920. One year father and Warner went on Thursday to the fair, for on that day there used to be a horse sale and my father intended to buy a horse. We kept running outside to see if they were returning and, after what seemed an eternity, father arrived, loaded with goodies from the fair, including our favourite brandy snaps. When he had unloaded, father told us he had bought a fine pony but it was not broken in and Warner was walking it home. We were very excited and quickly calculated how long it would take Warner to walk the five miles. Taking off the half-hour since father had left them, we decided it would be at least another three-quarters of an hour before they got home. How wrong we were, for only a few minutes later we heard hoofbeats coming down the road. A mad scramble from the tea table and we met them both in the yard. What a sight this pony was! A perfect gem, he looked a cross between a good racehorse and a Welsh mountain pony. Indeed, we learned afterwards he was from the Welsh mountains. While the adulation was going on, the pony was so hungry, he greedily ate from our hands. My brother said he had got tired of walking and, although it was risky to ride an unbroken pony with only a halter to control him, he had mounted the pony and trotted him home like a dream. We named him Bob and I fell for him hook, line and sinker.

By now I was sixteen and very anxious to help with the breaking in of Bob. He was easy to break in and it was not long before he was ridden and put between the shafts. He had only one fault: he loved to race away from us when we went to catch him. This exasperated my brother beyond endurance until his patience was exhausted. One day Warner was in a hurry and Bob was particularly wayward. At last we penned him into a corner where my brother thrashed him with a stick. This greatly upset the pony who never forgot this hiding and would not let any man catch him. After this I was always the one to catch him. I used to tempt him with lumps of sugar but quite often he would snatch the sugar and gallop away.

When the village gymkhana was held, we would enter Bob in three races. Often he would win the pony race and occasionally win the open race for all horses, but nearly every year he would win the musical chairs. Perhaps he had an advantage over the other horses because we loved to play this game with him in the home field. We children and our friends would spread sacks around the field, then all gather in the middle of the field and sing lustily. Warner would ride Bob around the field and, when we stopped singing, Bob would race to the sack he had chosen for himself. The pony enjoyed this game as much as we did and, when the musical chairs competition came at the gymkhana, he was raring to go.

The village butcher, Mr James, owned a beautiful high-stepping horse that had won many prizes at big shows. All contestants in the musical chairs had to follow this horse which would lead the procession round the field while the village band provided the music. Some of the riders hoped for a clearer start by lagging behind, but Warner would stay close to the leader and, instantly the music stopped, Bob would turn suddenly. Warner was aware of this practice and was ready. The horse galloped to the box of his choice and quite often would be there while the untrained horses at this game were being pulled up and turned around. The only time I remember him being beaten was when Warner tried to race Bob to a box of his choice and the pony wanted to go to another one.

One year I was standing at the ropes beside a little stout man. As the horses were parading, he observed: "What've they brought that fat, sweatin' 'oss for? That'll win nowt." I resented him belittling my beloved Bob, although he was both fat and sweating. At last I could stand it no longer. I nudged the man and said: "I'll bet you a shilling that pony will win two events and be in the first three of the open." The man looked at me pityingly, as though to ask what I knew about it. Bob won the pony race while he was still fresh and just managed to come third in the open. He was much distressed at the finish of the open and only his great heart got him there. After the adults' races he recovered sufficiently to win the musical chairs. I gave the offending man a nudge and asked him: "Now what about it?" but he answered never a word as I looked at him scathingly.

When I was around eleven, there was a great farm fire about a mile out of the village at Turnpost Farm. I was walking with two small children when we heard the ringing of the fire brigade bell and the galloping of horses. I have never forgotten the sight of those beautiful black galloping horses and that bright red vehicle with the shining brass on both the horses and the vehicle. All the men were in uniform with bright brass helmets. Those horses had galloped five miles from Loughborough and still had one more mile to go. Many years later there was another fire on the same farm. The ponds nearby were pumped dry, as there was no piped water. My eldest son caught fish trapped in the mud at the bottom of the turnpost pond.

Once a year, in November, the Quorn Hunt met in the village square where our school was situated. The headmaster allowed his pupils time from their lessons to see this impressive sight. We took out our forms, arranged them the length of the school wall and then stood on them to have a clear view of some of the best horses and riders in the country. On a sunny day the riders in their hunting pink were a spectacle to remember all one's life. One year the Prince of Wales, later King Edward VIII, attended the meet and this caused great excitement in the village. The children were quite awestruck at having a real prince to see. When they went back into class, the schoolmaster told them to write a composition on all they had seen that morning. He was reading my brother John's work over his shoulder when he suddenly gave John a hefty box on the ear, saying: "Don't you dare write such untruths about the Prince of Wales." My brother's feelings were hurt and he protested that he had written nothing but the truth. When the schoolmaster was marking the other compositions, he noticed that most of the other children had written the same story about the Prince of Wales and that it must be true. He apologized to John, promised to check the facts and, after much research, found that the boys were right in this delicate matter. John remembers what happened as vividly as if it had been yesterday. The Prince had eased forward in his saddle and urinated down his horse's shoulder, an act which was permitted by law only if it was unsafe to leave one's horse. The London cabbies blessed this law.

8 ANIMALS

During the summer months father had to travel two miles with a pony and float to milk our cows which were grazing so far away. He would wake me up at five-thirty in the morning to go with him to help round up the cows. They were milked in a small hovel which held only four cows at a time. They were milked in the same order every time; the cows knew that order and generally the next four would be waiting quietly for their turn to be milked. It is still surprising to me, a countrywoman, that cows always know their own place in a cowshed and, when they enter for milking, go straight to their own standing. When a new cow is brought into a herd, it causes trouble for the first few days at tying-up time, until it knows its own standing and is accepted by the other cows.

There was an old lady in the village, named Miss Dexter, who had several cows, blue and white in colour, which were always called the blue cows. They were the pride of the whole village when they walked to and from the common land where people with only one or two cows were allowed to graze their cattle during the summer months. Miss Dexter walked to the common land to milk the blue cows with a yoke over her shoulders and two huge buckets hanging at each. side. She must have been very strong, as two buckets full of milk are quite a weight. A man named Mr Hardy, who was a cripple, was paid a weekly sum to tent all these cows belonging to various people. It was quite a sight on the common at milking-time, for there would be nearly as many people milking as there were cows. A bowl of cow cake in a box was given to each cow to bring the milk down and the animals stood quietly, unchained, being milked.

One day it was sadly noticed that one of Miss Dexter's blue cows was becoming extremely thin. The vet diagnosed tuberculosis, which meant it had to be destroyed. In the course of the next few years all Miss Dexter's cows had to be destroyed because of this dreaded disease. Father, who admired the blue cows so much, had bought one of the heifer calves but it, too, died of the same disease when it grew to maturity. In due course every herd in the country had to have veterinary tests every six months for tuberculosis, until it was virtually exterminated. Butchers who slaughtered their own cattle had to have the meat compulsorily examined before it was allowed for sale. After the loss of her cows, poor Miss Dexter left her house and went to live in a much smaller place with just one field where she kept poultry. In her younger days when her parents were alive, Miss Dexter taught music but, after the loss of her cows, she seemed to lose heart. She never cleaned her house or even washed herself and the hens were allowed inside her house, roosting anywhere they could find, even on the piano. It was such a shame, for Miss Dexter was a very kind person and everyone in the village liked her.

To supplement his income during the First World War, father turned some of his buildings into a cowshed to hold ten cows. He rented a few acres for grass and hay but not sufficient to keep that number of animals. It was usual in those days for the different lanes leading from the village to be let for grazing during the summer. These lanes were, and still are, under the guardianship of the Feoffees, a group of responsible village gentlemen. Some time in the spring, a notice was posted in various parts of the village stating the night when the lane lettings would be auctioned to the highest bidder. My father was very short of grass, so he attended these meetings during the war and always bid the highest for the Burton on the Wolds and Hoton lanes which were the nearest to our home. When the cows were on the lane, someone had to be with them as they were loose; this was called 'tenting'. We children had to take turns at getting up early to tent the cows until around eight-thirty when they were put into the field. Then there was a race to get to school on time. When we came out of school, off we went to let out the cows on to the lane again to gently graze their way home in readiness for milking when father arrived home at five-thirty in the afternoon. Mother would give us our tea and then we would be ready to take the cows back to the field.

These journeys to and fro, grazing all the way, were a great help in supplementing the cows's feed. During the summer holidays we tented the cows all day from eight o'clock till four-thirty. Mother packed sandwiches and a bottle of water, there not being much else to drink during the war years. It was a lonely job as one never saw a car, only farmers carting hay and later corn, always of course with horses and carts. At that time tractors were unknown, at least in our part of the country.

The only man who drove a car was the vet who lived in Loughborough. The sight of this car was an absolute phenomenon and children stood transfixed watching it drive through the village, while the braver ones raced after it till it was out of sight. One day my sister Florrie and I were walking home from the next village of Rempstone where we had taken my father his dinner, as he was working there, when to our great astonishment a car drew up, the door opened and we were invited to ride the rest of the way home with the vet. We were speechless but gladly clambered in. The journey was over in a few minutes but, my word, did we have something to tell our friends.

Just after the war Warner started to keep ferrets, as he was now old enough to go rabbiting with father and he thought a few ferrets would be useful. Now whatever Warner wanted to do, I wanted to do as well, so when Warner started to build a little shed for the ferrets, I carried the bricks and helped all I could. The first ferret had a litter of seven. Six were that beautiful lemon colour and the seventh had dark brown fur, graduating down to pale lemon nearer the skin. I loved these ferrets and, although they smell a bit, they are very clean. I allowed them to creep all over me and I was never bitten once. I used to tease the ferrets with strips of meat. Once a ferret has a hold on anything, the only way to make it let go is to press a certain spot on its head and its jaws open automatically.

I used to let them get a good hold on the meat, then pressed the spot. I taught them to jump for their meat by holding it just out of their reach, edging it further and further away to make them jump higher.

As I was telling this story to an eighty-year-old lady living next-door, she shuddered and said that if she saw a ferret, she would die. I told her there was nothing to fear, as I let them creep around my neck. This she refused to believe, so I fetched our brown ferret, draped it round my neck and nonchalantly swaggered into her living room. To my horror the old lady went into hysterics. I had never seen anyone like that before. It frightened me to death, so I rushed home to mother who went to see her. When mother came back home, I was again in trouble. This escapade was not the only trouble the ferret caused me. The brown ferret was on my shoulder when I stood in front of the fireplace, over which a great mirror hung. Seeing itself in the mirror, the ferret jumped off my shoulder to fight its image. It had never seen a brown ferret before, only the plain yellow ones.

Another of my adventures with animals was with our terrier called Spot. I had a new pinafore which was a pink colour with a deep-red sprigged design. It was made on what we called a saddle or yoke. A lot of fullness was gathered on to this saddle with frills round the armholes and the bottom of the skirt. Mother asked me to take off my new pinny while I was playing after tea, but because I begged so hard to keep it on, she gave way, but with firm instructions to be careful not to get it dirty. I was extremely careful for a while until young Spot wanted a rough and tumble with me. I was completely lost and the dog and I rolled about together and raced around the orchard, Spot pulling at my new pinny, tearing another piece out of it at every pull. After the excitement was over, I began to count the cost and I knew I was in terrible trouble. I hung about the orchard, not daring to face my mother, chastising Spot most of the time, but as the dark hour approached, I had to face the music, When I entered the house, mother was very pleased to see me, as she had begun to wonder where on earth I had got to, but when she saw my

pinafore, or what was left of it, she was very upset, as a lot of sewing had gone into my new pinny. Although I was not smacked, I was sent straight to bed without any supper.

A dreadful thing happened to Spot. My father had taken him out on a shooting expedition and he was chasing a hare which ran off father's land on to that of a neighbouring farmer who shot the dog, breaking its leg. Father carried him home and put his leg into splints made from pieces of wood. After six weeks the splints were removed while we all watched with dread in our hearts, fearing it would not be a success. Spot walked very lame for a few weeks but in time was as good as new. Father had an awful row with his neighbour and they did not speak to each other after that for many years. However, when this farmer's stackyard caught fire, mother, father and the older children all took their place in line, passing buckets of water from all the pumps available.

When Warner was eighteen, he was allowed to take father's gun to shoot rabbits. One night it grew dark and Warner had not returned. Mother sent us other children to bed but certainly not to sleep, for we knew mother's fear and hatred of guns of any sort. Father went out over the fields where he thought Warner might have gone. He eventually found him lying down on some hay in an open-sided hovel with the gun beside him, its barrels pointing straight at his head. Father's first thought was: "My God, Warner has shot himself!" He ran to him and found that Warner had lain down to watch for a rabbit to come out and had fallen asleep. Father had previously lectured him about the handling of a gun and he was well and truly reprimanded.

When our baby brother Bill was around two years old, he and I had great fun on a bicycle father had helped me buy, which was brand-new and had cost three pounds seventeen and sixpence. The bike had a carrier on the back on which little Bill used to ride. We travelled miles and miles together on the bicycle, accident free, although by this time we were meeting the odd motor car. Mother allowed me to take the baby for these rides on one condition: I had to promise to get off every time we came to a crossroads. I loved having the baby with me, so I gladly agreed to do this and kept my word.

Our baby brother Bill could be naughty sometimes. During the spring when he was two and a half years old, father bought fifty day-old chicks and I was the one delegated to rear and look after them. Little Billie usually came with me to feed the chicks. We used to sit down on the grass, gradually throwing the food around us. This made the chicks very tame and they grew up unafraid of both Billie and myself. Suddenly we kept losing chicks, sometimes two or three a day, and the funny part of it was that the dead birds were always wet through. At last the penny dropped. Although Billie was under three years old, he was the only person apart from myself who could catch these birds quite easily. I kept a strict watch on the child and, sure enough, he toddled up the yard, into the orchard and sat down on the grass. The chicks immediately surrounded him and he quietly picked one up, took it to the horse trough, held it by its legs and dipped it into the water. Several times he held the poor chick up, watching it struggle for a while before immersing it again. When the struggling stopped, Billie said: "Mmm, he be deaded." At this point I ran out of hiding, took the chicken away from him – it eventually revived – and for the first time in his little life I spanked him soundly. He never did it again but I often wondered if he would have done, if I had not spanked him so soundly. I always feel an occasional spank at the right time does a lot of good.

About this time father bought two lovely young horses. One was a heavy shire, the other what we called a half-leg. The half-leg, which we called Bill, was to be broken in and used as a drayhorse. I lost my heart to him immediately on sight and spent so much time with him that we seemed to form an almost human understanding of each other. I groomed him continually, having been shown how by Warner. I spent hours on his back, both in the stable and while he was grazing in the orchard. Mother was afraid that this horse was much too big for me to manage, and when I had to fetch him from the field where he had been grazing, she gave me strict instructions not to ride him home. This was because he always shied at cars and motor bikes, for he hated them. He was especially frightened of the Brickhill engine bringing bricks to father's yard. I think this was the one and only time I deceived my mother, for I could not resist riding the horse most of the way home. I used to lead him out of the gate, close it, then draw him alongside the gate, climb it and spring on to his back. Then we were away for an exciting half-mile gallop. On reaching our street, I slipped off his back and walked him the rest of the way. I do not think any of my family ever found out about this escapade.

As time went on, we began to worry about this horse. He looked as fit as a fiddle, but one day Warner came home and reported that while chain-harrowing one of the fields, the horse had suddenly thrown up its head, then dropped like a stone. After struggling for a few moments, he got up and seemed perfectly alright, apart from a little trembling. Time went by and we had assured ourselves he was alright, when, as my brother galloped him home from the field, down he went again. I was following on my cycle and we both stood helplessly looking at the terrible struggling of our beloved Bill. He got up again and stood trembling for a very long time. We led him home and sent for the vet who examined him thoroughly but found nothing at all wrong with him. Quite a time went by without further incidents of this kind, until one day, when I was with him in the home field, the vet came roaring along the road on his motorbike. Bill threw up his head and shied away, racing to the middle of the field where he went down once again. I ran to the spot and sadly watched the horse's struggles, thinking he would soon be up again, but this time he lay still and I knew he was dead. I ran home sobbing to tell mother the dreadful news. She told me to go and tell Warner and father, who were working on a roof at the other end of the village. I took out my cycle and raced to deliver the awful news. I must have been incoherent in telling about poor Bill, for father nearly fell off the roof with shock: he thought I meant our little baby Bill had died.

The vet was called and a postmortem was done. The horse's body was cut from one end to the other and examined everywhere, but all was found to be perfect. Then the throat was cut open and a growth the size of an egg was found like a small ball on a string. Apparently most of the time this benign growth was doing no damage at all, but when the horse threw up its head, the growth fell over the breathing passage and he choked to death. Father was dreadfully upset at these findings, for he said the vet should have found this growth earlier and operated, cutting a few strands of sinew and releasing the blockage. The monetary loss from this horse was great but the loss for Warner and myself was immeasurable.

Living in the country, we got our sex education from animal behaviour. I remember how father used to ask one or two of us to help him separate one of our cows from the herd to take it to a certain farm. When we managed, after much trouble, to get it into the farmyard, we were curtly sent home. This happened from time to time to all our cows in turn. We kids were naturally curious and were not long in devising a way of finding out just what the secrecy was all about. After the farmyard gate was closed, nobody could see anything, as these gates were tall and made of strong wood, nothing like today's see-through iron gates. Instead of going home, we made a detour, coming back over the churchyard which was immediately opposite the farm gate. We then climbed a lime tree where we had a complete view of the whole farmyard. It also dawned on us that every cow we had taken to this farm had a calf nine months later.

A similar experience, this time with horses, gave us more knowledge. Every week during certain months of the year, a man came to the village, leading a magnificent black stallion, which he always took to the Three Crowns Inn where, in the field at the top of the yard, several great shire mares were waiting. We Nosey Parker kids used to hide behind a bed of nettles on the adjoining land to watch the proceedings. The mares would each be brought in their turn to the five-barred gate, where we noticed that, if the mare kicked at the stallion, the gate shielded him from grave injury and the mare was led away. The same procedure was followed until one of the mares made a great fuss of the stallion over the gate.

It was then opened and the two horses would mate. Our parents were determined we should not see these things but we quite often found ways and means of doing so. When dogs were mating in the street, we were fetched in, as my parents thought it wrong for children's eyes to see them.

The first vicar of Wymeswold to teach the village teenagers about sex was the Rev Edmunds about 1919. This instruction was given to the boys and girls who were about to be confirmed. First the boys' class was taken, then the girls'. The class was well and truly discussed throughout the village and very few of the parents really agreed with this outspoken way of teaching what our parents thought was a personal matter. A lighter side to these classes was also discussed freely. Apparently, during the girls' classes, the boys were curious to know what the girls were learning. They contrived to climb up on to the window ledges of the schoolroom and from this vantage point they overheard most of the conversation that was taking place. As I grow older and see the way young children are taught sex education in schools, I feel strongly there must be a midway course to educate our children. The way we learned about sex made us feel ashamed to talk about it. I was in my late teens before I realized that sex between two people who loved each other was a sacred and enjoyable happening, not something shameful that had to happen to create a baby.

9 THE WAR YEARS

During the First World War my father was left with only one old workman named Bill Wilson, who was a drummer in the Wymeswold Brass Band. He had a dreadful temper and we kids were frightened to death of him. However, we used to gang up on him and call names after him. "Old drummer Wilson, old drummer Wilson," we used to shout. We were always careful to keep a respectful distance because he was not particular about giving a right good hiding to the one he caught. Father did a little jobbing work during the war with the help of old Bill.

During the war we were to see an aeroplane at close quarters. Though we had never seen a plane before, we quickly realized this plane was in trouble and would have to be force-landed. Everyone on two feet who could run, ran and ran to the spot where it looked like landing and, by the time it eventually came down, quite half the young people of the surrounding villages were near enough to see it. Both the pilot and the plane were unharmed and a favoured few were allowed to sit in the plane.

Food became very scarce at the end of the war, although country people fared better than townspeople. During school time we were allowed to go and gather blackberries for preserving and rose hips to make syrup rich in vitamin C. The boys who were strong were given a patch of garden in which to grow vegetables for sale to parents. I think the money raised was given to the Red Cross. Father bought a couple of breeding sows which in the course of time provided food for many mouths. These pigs were made fat with whey from the cheese factory in the village, scraps if any, and small potatoes boiled in the copper and given to them once a day. We also had around fifty hens in one of the rented fields which were housed in an old road-caravan with nest-boxes down one side. One of the children had to walk half a mile every morning to give them their corn which was kept in an old iron receptacle in the caravan. At dark hour one of the older children went again to shut up the hens, so marauding foxes would not have an easy meal, and also to collect the eggs laid during the day. I do not think any mother these days would let a child walk that distance alone at dark hour, but we never gave a thought that anything dreadful would happen to us. Another food that helped a lot was cheese made from milk that went sour during the hot weather. This was called Colwick cheese; it was delicious when spread on bread with pepper and salt. So, with pigs, eggs, chickens, cheese, fruit and vegetables, we fared better than our town friends.

Father learned to kill the pigs himself and he salted down shoulders, sides and legs which lasted until the next pig was killed. Mother was kept busy with the rest of the pig, as she usually made fifteen to twenty pork pies which kept in perfect condition for up to three weeks, if the weather kept very cold. We have even eaten pork-pies one month old. Then sausage, faggots and haslet were made. All the spare fat was rendered down, which we called rendered lard. This lard enabled us to have home-made pastry all the year round. Our nearest and dearest were all given something from each pig: a porkpie, a few faggots, a bit of sausage, or what we called the fry, which consisted of pieces of liver, kidney, heart and something from inside the pig called skirting. This was like a frill which was put round the edge of the plate, then the meat and sweetbreads were arranged inside it. The effect was quite pretty and we kids looked forward to taking these titbits to our friends, because we were always given a copper or two. Brawn was made from the face and feet, and the leftover liquid made really good soup. When the pig was killed, one of father's workmen always came to catch the blood from the throat for black pudding and another took the stomach home for tripe. Boys in the village fought for the pig's bladder to blow up for a football. My father used to say that everything was used in a pig except its squeak.

Towards the end of the war, our market town of Loughborough was bombed by a German Zeppelin which was aiming at the gas works. Fortunately, the bombs missed, but a number of people were killed.

When the Great War was over and peace declared, every village had suffered terrible losses. In some families more than one member failed to return. Though some were badly wounded, others came through without a scratch and we gave thanks for those who had returned safely. Our workman, Bill Tomlinson, who fought all through the war, came home without a scratch, but he said war left its mark. He had got out of the habit of sleeping in a bed, so he slept on the floor for several nights. My own family did not suffer any of these great losses. Father was over age but had received his calling-up papers a few weeks before the Armistice. Warner was not old enough.

The peace rejoicing in Wymeswold took the form of a party for everyone. The village brass band marched around the streets, followed by all who could walk, while others sat at their doors watching the proceedings. Most people wore fancy dress. Games, races and all kinds of sports were enjoyed. After the war, life gradually began to get back to normal. The blackout was lifted but food supplies were slow in returning to pre-war standards.

When I was eleven years old, my father decided I was to learn to play the piano. A lady in the village, named Gladys Morrison, was the only person who taught piano playing. She had many pupils and was very successful in her profession. I was a reasonably good pupil but would never, as my father hoped, reach anywhere near the top. However, we did have enjoyable evenings song singing and on Sunday evenings hymn singing to my accompaniment. Later on I sat for exams and did moderately well.

Father was a hard taskmaster and, prior to my sitting these exams, he made me practise at least three hours a day. I became so sick of these exam pieces that my teacher said I was becoming stale, so after my three hours of practice she allowed me to play anything I liked. After timing three hours to the minute, I gaily started to play "Oh, will you wash my father's shirt? Oh, will you wash it clean? Oh, will you wash my father's shirt and wash it in margarine?" Before I came to the end of this little ditty, father burst into the room and knocked me clean off the piano stool, shouting: "Now play your set pieces." I told him that, after I had completed my set practice, Miss Morrison had given me permission to play anything I liked. My father was extremely hasty-tempered but was always very sorry when he was proved wrong.

Another time when I was unjustly punished was when mother accidentally trampled on my father's bare toes; he thought it was me and I got the clout. Mother was upset and explained it was her fault. I said: "Now Dad, what are you going to do about it?" He gave me that whimsical smile of his and said: "The next time you deserve a good hiding, remember you have had it." Sure enough, it was not long before I was in need of chastisement and, as father raised his hand, I raised both mine and shouted: "I've had it, Dad. I've had it, you know." He grinned and that was the end of that.

Unlike father, mother very rarely lost her temper. Although there were nine of us living at home, our house was always clean and tidy. "I just cannot have you children leaving all your things around," she said. "There is a place for everything and everything must be in its place." Our boots always had to be placed under a sofa, starting with the eldest at the head end and gradually working down to the baby's boots. When we were in a hurry in the morning, each of us knew just where to dive to grab our own boots. In the living-kitchen were two rows of pegs on the wall, the top row for my parents and the bottom row for the younger ones. I would pester mother for the use of a top peg, for I thought that was a sign of prestige, but I never got one, even when I was older, because I was so small. My sisters Lottie and Edna did not seem to mind having pegs on the bottom row, for they were easy-going. When Edna was little, mother used to say that if Edna had a ball to play with, she would sit on the rug, throw away the ball and wait for someone else to give it to her back.

I loved darning and when at the age of eleven I was allowed to darn most of the family's socks and stockings, I felt very proud. However, as I grew older, I resented darning Edna's stockings while she sat reading, and one week I left her two pairs undarned. Mother questioned me as to why I had left Edna's stockings and I said I was not going to do her darning while she read. Mother replied: "Oh yes you will. Now do as you are told." I said that I had darned the family's stockings since I was eleven, so Edna could darn her own at the age of thirteen. From then on, Edna darned her own stockings. She also became adept at embroidery work, much better than I who was a good sewer but never achieved anything like Edna's standard of embroidery.

At an early age I showed signs of what I wanted to do when I left school. When asked about this by the school's inspector, I answered that I wanted to be a schoolteacher or a dressmaker in that order. My chance of becoming the former was completely wrecked when mother refused to let me sit the scholarship exam for the Loughborough High School. The schoolmaster had been to see her and told her I would "walk it" and he would give me extra tuition free of any charge. My heart nearly stopped beating with suspense waiting for mother's answer, but she regretfully said a definite "No". The headmaster said I would benefit from a secondary education and ought to have it, but still the reply was "No". Mother's greatest fear was that at the age of eleven, in all weathers and alone, I would have to cycle five miles to Loughborough. The other worry was that father could not afford to send all his children to secondary school. She said: "We cannot do for one what we cannot do for the others." The teacher came once again, but mother was adamant, and I left school at the age of thirteen, crying my eyes out.

Just before I left school, the first ever bus service started coming through our village. This enabled us to travel to Nottingham and Loughborough in a quarter of the time it used to take. Many amusing incidents took place in those early bus-riding days. On the way home from Nottingham there was a very steep hill called

Bunny Hill, and sometimes, especially in frosty weather, the bus stalled. Then all the strong passengers would alight and they helped by pushing at the back, which usually got the bus safely to the top.

Some of the Wymeswold teenage boys used to walk the two miles to Rempstone, then under cover of darkness, when the bus slowed up on the Rempstone Hill, they climbed up the ladder on the side of the bus which was used for putting luggage on to the roof. They rode on top of the bus all the way to Wymeswold where, for a time, they managed to hop off before the lady conductor opened the door for the passengers to alight. This escapade ended when the conductress, who had been informed about it, was at the open door ready and waiting. As each boy came down the ladder, his posterior received a whacking kick.

In those early days it was not unusual for passengers to ask the driver to wait a few minutes. One day my father asked me to watch out for the bus, as he was taken short and would have to go. I was terribly embarrassed when I asked the driver if he would wait a few minutes and he asked me why. The why was obvious when all the passengers watched my father running from the outside closet, pulling up his trousers as he ran.

For threepence one could put quite a large parcel on the bus and it would be delivered at a certain house where one could collect it at one's leisure. Once I remember seeing an armchair delivered to Wymeswold, but that was met and the owner helped the driver to get it out through the narrow door. These free-and-easy days are over now.

10 TEENAGE YEARS

My first job was in Loughborough with my sister Florrie. I cycled to work at the Zenobia scent factory, where I learned to make fancy boxes to hold the bottles of scent. I earned 12/6d a week and quite liked the work, but I soon realized that girls working "on their own time" earned much more than I did. I plucked up my courage and asked the overlooker if I might do the same and she agreed to see about it. This meant that one received a certain figure per gross for a certain type of box. After a month I was allowed to go on my own time and the first week I earned 24/6d, very nearly double the flat rate. I had been there six months when a lot of workers were short-timed. I worked next to a girl who was lazy, repeatedly late and altogether a bad worker. One Friday, when the manager gave us our pay packets, he gave us both a week's notice. I just looked at him and, I must admit, very sarcastically I said: "Thank you." He turned back sharply and asked: "What did you say, Miss?" "Thank you," I said. Without another word he left us, but the following Monday morning he came up to me and told me to disregard the week's notice. He said: "I wouldn't get rid of you for anything, but I just had to get rid of your table-mate." He said I was to take three weeks off, then return, as he did not really want to lose me. I was pleased to hear this but, although the room overlooker came to Wymeswold to ask me to return, I never went back. My parents had decided to let Lottie go out to work and I had to take her place as mother's help at home. In fact, I was father's help, too, as I loved being outside on the farm, or rather smallholding. By this time we had left our old house, which had been let to the village schoolmaster, and had moved into Grandfather Wootton's house with around twenty acres of grassland. The building materials were all moved to this place and my grandparents moved to one of the new cottages my grandfather had built a few years earlier.

Our new house had been built by my grandfather and, although it had four bedrooms, it did not have a bathroom, so we still bathed in the same old way. In the back kitchen, however, there was a water pump and a copper to heat the water, so we were one step nearer to a bathroom, as we did not need to heat our water outside in the old washhouse. Our bath was a long wooden tub, out of which the water used to trickle in the summer because the wood used to shrink, but it never leaked in winter.

I was thirteen before I saw the sea and fifteen before I had a holiday at the seaside. Lottie and I both earned and saved five pounds each and we went to Skegness, our nearest seaside resort. We travelled on a crowded train and, although Lottie had a seat, I sat on my case, as did many others, in the corridor of the train. Mother packed us off with a dressed chicken and various cookies and then we were on our own, buying all we needed. In those days people like ourselves bought their own food and the lady of the boarding house would cook it for us along with all the other boarders' vegetables which we all shared. Lottie and I saw our first film, called *If Winter Comes*. It was so sad we both cried unashamedly. I whispered to Lottie: "Are you, sniff, are you, sniff, enjoying it, Lottie?" "Yes, sniff. Are you, Nell?" "Sniff, oh yes," says Nell, "I really am," tears rolling down my face. All that cost us sixpence each. When we got to bed that night, we found we had caught fleas from the cinema. We set to and tried to catch them, but in the morning we were well and truly marked on our bodies. We enjoyed our first holiday, but we were not spent out, for we both took home nearly a pound each from our original fund of five pounds, and we had bought small presents for each of the family.

Father and Warner would have a few days' holiday together but mother had been married for over twenty years before she and father managed to arrange a holiday together. Our friend Miss Simpson offered to sleep at our house, after she had closed her shop, and Florrie took a week's holiday to look after the family. Our parents spent a week at Blackpool together, a holiday they both enjoyed. Every one of us received a present from Blackpool, which made us hope they would take a holiday again the next year, but although father begged mother to go, it was many years before she consented to go to Skegness with him. She said she was happiest at home. Bless her, she was such a home-loving person.

During our teenage years my young brother John thought he would like to start making wine. He was very successful and our cellar, which stored only potatoes and junk, was cleaned out thoroughly to provide a good place for his wine. Our family drank wine and intoxicants only at parties and at Christmas, and then not until we were eighteen. My parents thought home-made wine was a little different and John needed no encouragement before he offered our visitors a glass of his own make. Once he had made a new lot of wine, probably up to eight gallons, and when most of it was bottled, there he found, lying in the bottom of the pancheon, a dead mouse. A great debate followed. Would the wine be fit to drink? Would the wine be contaminated by the dead mouse? How long had the mouse been there? John hated to think about all his trouble being ruined by a tiny mouse, but in the end he emptied all the bottles of wine down the kitchen sink.

John tells the story about one of father's friends, John Smith – my future father-in-law – who came to our house every Friday night to do business. Mr Smith was secretary and father was treasurer of the Oddfellows Club. People paid into this club so much money a week, then if they were ill, they drew a certain amount of money each week until they were fit to work again. As National Insurance stamps became law, this club gradually ran down. To continue the story of the wine, one Friday night when he came, Mr Smith was feeling ill. He thought he was developing flu, so father asked John to give his visitor a big glass of his home-made wheat wine. After a time Mr Smith said: "I am going to be very rude, John, and ask for another glass of your wine. I feel warmer now than I have felt all day." John gave him another glass but this extra wine caused him trouble, for Mrs Smith accused John of getting her husband tipsy. On his way home in the dark Mr Smith had been a little unsteady on his legs and had stepped into the brook, saturating his trousers,

When I was in my teens, our new village hall was built. It was the finest hall for miles around and people flocked to whist drives and dances for many years. By this time motor cars were more frequent on our country roads and transport to these festivities was much easier. Our dances were so popular, our hall was full to overflowing. An extremely energetic committee worked to pay off the debt owed to the hall trustees. Two ladies started Friday night hops which were enjoyed by all. Younger people who could not dance were welcomed and were taught the basic steps by the two ladies and other experienced dancers. The hall committee bought two billiard tables, dart boards, a table-tennis table, packs of cards and other games such as dominoes. The fellowship in our village during those years after the war was marvellous and rarely did we have any trouble.

When I was around fifteen years old, I was asked by Mrs Hall and Mrs James, the two ladies who arranged the hops, if I would take turns with Mrs Hall in playing the piano for the dancing, as at seventy years of age she was getting very tired. I knew this meant that I could dance only half the dances, but Mrs Hall had played for so many years for the young people's benefit that I could not refuse. We had been quite happy to dance to her old-fashioned tunes, but I decided to introduce some modern ones if I could save enough money to buy the music. It was a surprise when I found these cost only sixpence each, so I gradually bought music for several dances. Sometimes tunes such as "Does the spearmint lose its flavour on the bedpost overnight?" and "Mother's got a pimple on the tip of her nose" were considered acceptable, but "In Riky's cowshed last night" and "We must have one more yum-tum-tum before we go away" were thought indecent and suggestive. The latter was a popular quickstep that Mrs Hall particularly hated. Once, when I was playing it, the dancers would not sit down and encored it over and over again. Eventually Mrs Hall came on to the stage and snatched the music from the piano. This caused an uproar and the dancers, much to my sorrow, booed Mrs Hall. One realizes that, even in the 1920s, the young people sometimes acted inconsiderately to the old, even when they had done so much for them. Eventually Mrs Hall retired from playing for dancing, but she still came and had a dance occasionally. Two other young girls, Kathleen Smith and Madge Peel, took their turns at the piano, which enabled the hops to continue.

The neighbouring village of Hoton had now built a fine new hall, but not nearly so grand as Wymeswold's. Our walks to dances in the nearby villages were almost as much fun as the dances. We never seemed to be tired, even after walking the two miles there, dancing until 2 a.m. and then romping home another two miles. At this time the slow waltz became popular, pushing the old-time waltz down the scale. The quickstep and the foxtrot came second and third in popularity. Suddenly all England was taken by storm: the Charleston had arrived. We teenagers were anxious to learn this crazy dance but did not know quite how to set about it. Fortunately a Nottingham cousin of one of our crowd came to spend a holiday in Wymeswold. She danced the Charleston almost professionally, so we asked her to teach it to us at one of our hops. She asked us all to bring a chair each and stand behind it, holding on to the back. Without the music she said: "Now all of you pretend you are putting out a cigarette on the floor." We thought this was easy, but when we tried to do the same to music, changing feet to each beat, we were hopeless. The fun it caused was really hilarious. After a time a few of us got the rhythm and at later hops taught some of the others, though some never did master it. We also had party dances. The Palais glide was danced in rows across the room, unlike the Congo where we followed one another round the room, holding the shoulders or waist of the dancer in front. Bumps-a-daisy and the Lambeth Walk seemed to take the place of the polka, but the lancers reigned supreme in our village for many years. The teenagers of today miss the thrill of dancing this energetic, exhilarating dance – I loved it. The barn dance, the veleta, the Saint Bernard's waltz and the military two-step faded a little but never entirely. I had a favourite dance called the Maxina, danced with what was called the 'open hold', with the gentleman standing slightly behind the lady, holding her hands over her shoulders.

Once, after my marriage, when my husband and I attended the Loughborough Farmers' Ball, the Maxina was requested. The band played several sequences, but nobody got up despite the tradition that the requesters started the dance. It soon became obvious this was not their intention so, as our feet were itching to dance our favourite Maxina, we plucked up our courage and went on to the floor alone. To our great embarrassment nobody else took the floor. We were alone in that huge ballroom which seemed to us the size of a field. When we finished the dance, the clapping would not stop until we had danced the Maxina again. During the repeat performance we were joined by the couple who had requested the dance. They told us afterwards that they had not dared start the dance, as they were unsure of the sequences.

Ten years later I was waiting for a bus in Nottingham, when I noticed a lady who kept looking at me. I asked her if I should know her and her answer was: "No, but I remember you dancing the Maxina with your husband at the Loughborough Town Hall." She told me that my dress had been an elegant wine-coloured ring velvet, a velvet so soft it could be drawn through a ring, and that we had danced beautifully. I appreciated this lady bothering to tell me all this and I thanked her for the compliment before we went to catch our different buses.

Although we now had our village hall, the church and the church schoolroom still remained the centre of our social life. John Taylor, our new organist, who later became my sister Florrie's husband, arranged many sacred entertainments, mostly held in the church which had a fine organ. One Friday evening the church choir, which included some good singers, sang *Olivet to Calvary*, which we had practised all through the previous winter. My sister Florrie sang the soprano solo, I sang contralto and my brother Warner the baritone. The tenor was sung by John Peel who sang in the choir for over fifty years. The Brown family, who kept the Post Office, was especially talented. The father was a bass singer, the mother a treble, the elder son a baritone and the younger son a tenor. Later their daughter Connie became one of the best soprano singers in the county. Her parents had her voice trained by the best tutors they could find. For years her beautiful powerful voice enthralled her audiences. Connie gave her services free for fundraising charities and it was with great sadness that we learned she had contracted tuberculosis. Fortunately she recovered but her voice lost some of its power, although she still sang beautifully.

At the village hall a boys' club was formed and one of the trustees used to give his time, in turn with others, to keep order, though rarely did any trouble occur. There seemed little for the young girls to do, so along with a few boys they called a meeting in the hall to see if anything could be arranged. A tennis court was proposed, a committee was formed and work started to raise funds. We had socials, dances, garden parties, raffles; anything and everything we could think of was tried and eventually enough money was raised to finance one court which had to have an especially high wire fence, as the court was next door to garden allotments.

I loved this game but never attained more than fourth or fifth place in our team. My sister Edna was also a very keen player and we were about equal as regards prowess. One game with Edna I shall never forget. I had pestered her that day against her will for a complete set of tennis. She was trying on a new pair of stays, the kind where the laces are pulled tighter and tighter until they really hug the figure. Her bargain was that, if I would lace up her stays, she would play tennis with me. It was very hot that summer's day and halfway through our game, which I was winning, Edna shouted: "Our Nell, you have tightened my stays too tight and you have done it on purpose so you could beat me."

In the summertime tennis took precedence over any other sport with us teenagers. None of us owned a car, so we rode our bicycles to and fro to other clubs outside the village. The furthest we travelled was about ten miles to a large village called Ruddington, over the border into Nottinghamshire. This we thought a swanky club, really snobbish. Instead of this putting us off our game, however, their attitude put us all on our mettle. On one occasion, loud enough so I could hear, the girl in their number one couple said: "Gracious, are we expected to play school kids now?" The number one couple for Wymeswold was a fourteen-year-old High School girl named Madge Peel, who had excelled at tennis in her form, and my kid brother Bill who had played ball at a wall continuously for hours on end until he was fourteen, old enough to be allowed to join the club. The game came easily to him and he was soon beating all the men in our club. This sarcastic remark about playing school kids irritated me considerably and, knowing our young couple's skill, I challenged the Ruddington girl to a bet of one shilling that our school kids would beat their number one couple. In the best of nine games, our youngsters beat them nine-love.

A team we particularly enjoyed playing was Upper Broughton which had some of the best sports one could ever wish to meet. Through the years of growing older, we played bowls with those same wonderful people.

11   DRESSMAKING

When I was sixteen years old, my parents decided I should learn dressmaking and tailoring. Mother was successful in obtaining a place for me with a Miss Fisher of Loughborough. Edna stayed at home in my place to help mother in the house and to do light jobs on our smallholding, which father still ran as a sideline to his building trade.

Miss Fisher had gained an excellent reputation in the town for dressmaking and I was told I was a lucky girl to be taking my apprenticeship with her. I was apprehensive about such a change of environment because for the previous two years I had led a carefree open-air life with a tremendous amount of physical activity. I decided that, if I cycled the five miles to Loughborough and back, I would at least get some exercise. I started from home on my cycle at 7-45 in the morning to arrive at work by 8-30. Then I worked until six in the evening, with one hour for dinner. This meant I had to sit sewing eight and a half hours a day for five days a week and four and a half hours on Wednesdays. I loved the sewing part of my work but missed my life of freedom at home. Eventually I got used to it and was quite determined to make a good dressmaker. I earned five shillings a week, less insurance contributions. Mother told me that she would not charge me any money for my board and she would pay for two of my dinners during the week. Dinners cost a shilling for meat with two vegetables and threepence more if one had a sweet, Needless to say, I always had a sweet. On other days Miss Fisher's sister reheated a dinner saved by mother from the previous day. For a sweet on those days, I nipped into the cake shop next door and spent twopence on a cream horn or a jam puff.

After around a year of my apprenticeship I was promoted to do a little shopping for sundries and matching materials for trimmings. I enjoyed this bit of responsibility, for it enabled me to get out into the open air. I always said that, had it not been for the cycling, I could never have stayed with Miss Fisher.

I had lots of escapades on my bicycle. Once I was cycling merrily along, when a man came out of his yard which was a blind alley. I was going downhill and I braked so hard that over the handlebars I went. The fall shook me badly, but I was able to finish my journey to work. On another day I saw a boy travelling unconcernedly along without holding his handlebars. I thought this was extremely clever, so I started to practise this myself, becoming really good at it. I determined to ride all the way to Loughborough without touching my handlebars, so l travelled through the village and up the hill towards Hoton. When I released my hands, everything went well, but when I reached Hoton, I faced a very tricky turn on to the main road. Luckily nobody was around and I managed it quite well, then it was downhill all the way to Loughborough. When I reached the Brush works, I thought: "I have done it." I was so proud and was bursting to tell them all at home. What did I get, though? No congratulations as I expected, but from father: "You damn fool, Nell! Don't ever do that again." One must realize that there was little traffic on the roads in those days. Now it would be nightmarish to attempt anything like it. Another foolhardy trick we used to do was to catch on to the back of a lorry and let it pull us along. I hope when my grandchildren read this, they will not try to emulate their silly old grandma, for it was dangerous then and it would be a hundred times more so now. Lorries travel so fast these days, but when I was young, they went at about twenty miles an hour.

Mother once asked me to cycle to the next village where a farmer had set one of his fields with strawberries which cost fourpence a pound. When I arrived home, mother prepared the fruit for tea but she thought: "There is never four pounds of fruit here." So she weighed the strawberries, stalks and all, and the total was only just over three pounds. "Oh dear," thought I, "I'm in trouble again." "Now, Nell," said mother, "take these strawberries back and tell the farmer he has made a mistake on the weight. Ask him to weigh them again." I looked at mother and told her I could not do that, because I had been eating them all the way home. I was reprimanded and, of course, I had no strawberries and cream for tea.

Our road from Wymeswold to Hoton was only a dirt road and in winter it became a quagmire, which made cycling to work extremely hard. The worst journey I remember was when there had been a snowstorm lasting all day. A severe frost had hardened the ground like iron. A friend who also lived in Wymeswold and worked in Loughborough, waited for me at the Brush works entrance, so we could ride home together. Her name was Florrie Tyler. She was a big girl, very strong indeed, and her company, especially that night, was greatly appreciated. The snow was still coming down thick and fast and, with these blizzard conditions, we were appalled at the prospect of the journey ahead. We went along as well as could be expected for the first mile, then it was uphill all the way to Hoton. In fact, the hill was called the Long Hill, a matter of nearly three miles. We met no one and no one passed us. The wind was so strong going up that hill, it fetched us off our cycles time and time again. We could hardly see for the blinding snow and quite often we had to get off and walk. That journey to Hoton took us nearly three hours and we still had the worst two miles to go over the rutted road to Wymeswold. When we had covered the first part which was on the level, we came to a slight rise which seemed to us like Everest, for we were both quite exhausted. My friend stumbled off her cycle and, clutching her handlebars, said: "Nell, I'm buggered. I can't go any further." I had never heard my friend swear before, but it was understandable, as we were both stone cold. Snow had frosted on our clothing and we were desperately hungry, too, not having eaten since midday, I tried hard to encourage her to make the last great effort, reminding her that, if we could make the next few hundred yards, it would be downhill the rest of the way home. I am quite sure also that, had my friend not waited for me, neither of us would have made it home that night. We are still friends and often recall that worst journey of all journeys, which took nearly four hours of the hardest slogging I have ever known. Mother was frantic with worry. She stood at the door, dressed in her warmest clothing, waiting for me. When she saw and heard my cycle coming up the yard, she said a prayer of thankfulness. I well remember her saying: "Child, child, thank God you are home." I was bundled inside, helped off with my frozen garments and set before the fire with my feet in hot mustard water. This was mother's cure-all: the slightest cold and it was feet in mustard and water. After I was warmed, I was given a hot meal on my knee and put to bed with a warm oven shelf to keep me warm. On cold nights mother used to put firebricks in the oven until they were really hot, and then they would be wrapped in flannel and placed in the bed ten minutes before we climbed between the sheets, then we used to push them lower down to keep our feet warm. Mother had some wonderful ideas, handed down no doubt from her own mother.

When we children went to school with thick sloppy snow on the ground, mother would cover our boots with father's old socks. Then she would tell us to run as fast as we could to school, so our boots would not be so wet. We had no Wellingtons in my childhood days. Plastics and polythene were not invented then. Oil heaters were put in bedrooms in extreme weather.

After I had finished my apprenticeship, I would have liked to have set up my own dressmaking business in my own village, but I could not see my way clear. Although our house had four bedrooms, all were in use and I could not ask my parents for the use of their sitting room. I was living at this time at the house of Miss Simpson from the little shop. She had lost her aunt, Miss Wood, and was managing the shop on her own but doing no sewing. She was just a little nervous of sleeping on her own, probably because of the shop money around, and my sister Florrie had slept at her house after the death of Miss Wood. When Florrie left the village to work in Nottingham, I was asked to take her place. We were talking one evening about the possibility of setting up a business on my own. Miss Simpson also thought it would be a splendid idea. I could earn six times more money than I was earning with Miss Fisher, but I was disconsolate for I could not think how this ambition could be managed. A month or so went by, when Miss Simpson, whom by now we all called Aunt Becky, said to me one night: "Nell, I want to show you something upstairs." She took me through the shop, then upstairs to the storeroom above. When she opened the door of her old dressmaking room and said: "Nell, it is all yours; you only need a sewing machine and a table", I was absolutely stunned by her amazing goodness and for a time I was speechless. Then she said: "Do you like it, Nell?" "Like it?" I answered, "I think it is just perfect." I asked how much the rent would be and Aunt Becky replied: "Nothing in money, but I wondered if you would keep shop for me while I take a holiday with my sister who lives at Wisbech." I was sure I would be able to manage the shop, for while sleeping there, I had helped quite a bit. Aunt Becky said she had prepared this old sewing-room for me because she loved me like a daughter. My sleeping at her house had been a joy to her and she treasured the hour or so we spent together chatting before going to bed. I thanked her for her kindness and gladly promised to do all I could to help in the shop. I sat down in the sewing-room dumbstruck. I just could not believe that I was going to start on my own in this room that Aunt Becky had decorated in her spare time. What a Herculean task for a woman who ran a shop of that size entirely on her own. Needless to say, the next thing was to buy a new sewing machine, a treadle one which cost seventeen pounds ten shillings. I had not had the chance to save much money, as I was earning only 12/6d per week from Miss Fisher. I had done a lot of other sewing, but it was mostly for my family, who did not pay me anything, because I did not pay any board to mother. That had been the agreement right from the start of my dressmaking course. Father helped me buy the machine by making up the money that I was short of. Miss Fisher was upset when I gave in my notice, for she hoped I would stay on with her. She offered to double my wages, but I could not accept. She said that, if I did not get enough work to keep me in full time, she would be pleased to have my help at any time, even if only for one day a week. Fortunately, this occurred only once when I went back for one week, which I enjoyed immensely.

When I was working with Miss Fisher, I made myself a navy blue coat and went to work in it, to show it off a bit. Miss Fisher, who was a person who rarely gave any praise, asked me who had made my new coat. I told her I had made it myself. She then asked who had done the collar and reveres and who had fitted and put in the sleeves. When I told her I had done the work myself, she quietly said: "Right. In future you do all our collar and reveres work and put in as many sleeves as possible. You have done both of these better than I could myself." This was indeed great praise, but I omitted to tell her that I had been receiving lessons from a reputable tailor on how to do this particular work.

On the advice of a friend I had leaflets printed, advertising that Ellen Wootton was setting up a dressmaking business in Clay Street. These were taken round to every house in Wymeswold and the surrounding villages. This publicity proved worthwhile: on the day I started I had six weeks of work in hand. The order that really set me on my feet was the wedding outfits of one of my friends, a second cousin called Harriet Bryans (whose elder daughter was to marry my eldest son twenty-five years later). This order was for a white crêpe de Chine dress for the bride, which was made with a hip-length bodice, very fashionable in the 1920s, with boxed pleats smocked down the skirt for about eight inches, the pleats flowing from the smocking to a mid-calf length. There were four brides-maids, two of whom were small children. Their dresses were periwinkle blue, a delightful colour which enhanced their colour-ing, for all were black-haired girls with lovely complexions. In addition to the bridal dresses, I made seven dresses for guests at the wedding. I worked on this order from early morning until late at night. Of course, for this wedding I felt it was a must to have a new dress myself. I chose a petunia coloured crêpe de Chine material, which I sent away to have accordion-pleated. I fitted these pleats to a yoke and round the waist I wore a multicoloured richly embroidered band which toned with the dress. I loved this outfit as it seemed to flatter my dark skin and my black hair. I was very proud to see my work at this wedding and I received many congratulations from the wedding guests, but what pleased me most was a comment I overheard outside the church. A complete stranger remarked that she had never seen a prettier wedding and asked who had made the dresses. I learned afterwards that this lady held a responsible position in a good class dress-shop.

When I had saved a little money, I was able to obtain patterns of material from which my customers could choose, and I bought wholesale sundries that were often used in dressmaking. This was an added income, well worth while as on very good materials I would be allowed two shillings a yard discount. All the Loughborough shops allowed me a discount if my customers were with me when they bought their materials. These few shillings seem ridiculous compared with the cost of clothing today, but during my early career as a dressmaker they were quite substantial. My income during my best week's dressmaking came to six pounds which meant extremely long hours of work. Quite often I would work eleven hours a day, occasionally more.

During the odd week that was not filled with dressmaking, I made my father's shirts. He wore a grey flannel one underneath a striped flannelette one; both were made very long, reaching to mid-calf. I thought this was very old fashioned and each year I made his shirts one inch shorter. After about three years I overheard him complaining to mother that materials shrank more than they used to. Mother said: "Such rubbish! Of course they don't." 'Well," father remarked, "all I can say is that our Nell is cutting them shorter each new shirt she makes." I was accused of this and, of course, had to admit it was so. I was told that in future I was to go back to the original length.

Which reminds me of a dress I made out of two remnants of different materials. Mini-skirts had become the fashion, so I made the dress-length two or three inches above the knee. Father looked at my new dress and said: "You can lengthen that dress, Nell, before I shall allow you to go out in it." "I'm sorry, father, I can't, as there is no hem to let down. Besides, short skirts are fashionable and, seeing I'm a dressmaker, I must keep in the fashion or I shan't get any work." Reluctantly he gave way and allowed me to wear my new mini-dress. Mini-skirts became fashionable once again during the 1960s.

12   COURTSHIP

In 1922, when my brother Warner attained his majority, mother gave him a splendid party. She was a marvellous party giver, remembering so many games from her youth which we enjoyed immensely. During that memorable party, although I was only a month short of sixteen, I fell in love with one of my brother's friends. John Sidney Smith was the son of lifelong friends of my parents. He was a seventeen-year-old handsome boy with dark wavy hair. That night I knew with certainty he was the boy I would like to marry. I did not think I stood much chance, for I was not particularly good-looking, rather small and young-looking for my age. I had jet-black hair, straight as a yard of pump water, or so my mother said, and a very tanned skin full of small freckles because of my open-air life. Although I was an outgoing kind of girl, I had no idea how to set about getting noticed by this young man, and there were many pretty girls in the village running after him. My sister Florrie was certainly attractive to boys, for she always had some boy running after her. Florrie was much better looking than I, with great dark-brown eyes and a lovely complexion.

On the Christmas Eve after Warner's twenty-first party, I came into contact with Sid Smith again while carol singing. It was a bitterly cold night and thick frosted snow covered the ground, but we were young and enjoyed the mile and a half walk to one of the largest farms just outside the village, where we always sang and were invited in for coffee and mince pies. Later in the evening, or rather in the early hours of Christmas morning, our last call was at Mr James, the butcher's. He always gave us wine. Now none of us was used to drinking wine and most of the carollers became very happy. I hated the stuff and one glass of sherry was enough to make my head swim. I miserably looked on while the others were larking about and Sid Smith was kissing all the girls but me. However, to my great surprise, he asked if he could see me home. Though I knew my parents would disapprove, I whispered: "Yes." On the way home he put his arm round me and, when we were half-way home, he stopped and tried to kiss me. Though I was small, I was exceedingly strong and wiry enough to evade his kisses. After a time Sid became so cross because of my refusal that he pushed me away from him saying: "Right. You won't kiss me, you can walk home by yourself." And, much to my chagrin, that was exactly what I did. Florrie was waiting for me to arrive home. She was cross with me because she had received strict instructions to see me home safely and dared not go inside without me at three o'clock on Christmas morning. When I climbed into my bed, I thought: "Nell, my girl, you've well and truly botched everything. He will never ask you home again."

I was wrong, however, for a few days before my sixteenth birthday, a whist drive was held in our schoolroom. Mostly the older generation attended the whist drive and, at around ten-thirty in the evening, the room was cleared for dancing for all ages. Sid Smith was a good dancer but at that time I had not made much progress in that line. He did not ask me to dance but he did ask to take me home. Unfortunately, my parents would not allow me out alone with boys and had arranged for a sixty-year-old friend of mother's to see me safely home. I did not want Sid to know of this ban and preferred him to think I had been asked by another boy. So I turned up my nose and told him: "No, thank you. Someone else is taking me home." Sid told me in later years that it was my refusal to allow him to kiss me that attracted his attention, as I was the first girl ever to refuse, and he vowed to himself that in the end I would kiss him.

Another time Florrie and I had been singing solos in the Good Friday service, after which Sid and another boy asked us to go for a walk along the footpaths on the land his father farmed – to hear the nightingales sing, they said. Florrie unhesitatingly said "Yes" and, of course, I went along as well. Whom should we meet but Sid's mother, talking to a friend outside their farmhouse gate. Now I was only sixteen and I wished the ground would open and swallow me up before we reached his mother, but she just looked at us rather sternly and wished us "Good evening". When we arrived home, our mother asked us where we had been. "The service can't have lasted that long surely," she said. When we told her we had been for a walk with two boys, she asked: "What boys?" We told her their names and mother said: "Florrie can go out with boys, but not you, Nellie, not until you are eighteen years old." That was two years away and it seemed an awfully long time to wait. The only time I saw Sid was at choir-practice, but he was not allowed to see me home, and after the Sunday night service it was the same – "Come straight home, Nellie."

By this time I knew Sid was beginning to feel something for me and he became very friendly with my brother Warner. Again he told me later that getting friendly with Warner was the only way he could think of to keep in touch with me. During the summer we played cricket in our home field and in the winter Sid used to come and play cards with the family. I was no whist player but was persuaded by Sid to join in their game. Mother loved this game and attended every whist drive she could. I did not really like the game, but it was wonderful sitting opposite Sid, surreptitiously having a shy glance at him when he was not looking. When he started pressing my foot under the table, I knew I was on my way to gaining his affections. He would often ask me if he could take me home from choir practice, or after the Sunday night service, or take me to the pictures, or to a dance in one of the surrounding villages, and I always had to say "No". This went on for over a year until one day, after watching a cricket match, Sid followed me out of the grounds and asked me to go to the pictures with him the following Saturday night. When I gave him the usual negative answer, he took hold of me by both arms and said he would not let me go until I had told him why I would not go out with him. I looked straight at him and gulped out: "My mother won't let me. She says I'm not old enough." He answered by saying: "Right. I will wait until your mother will let you." He turned and went straight back to the cricket match, leaving me feeling both jubilant and despondent: jubilant because he had said he would wait for me, despondent because the time seemed so long before I became eighteen.

He kept his word and stopped taking other girls out. Brother Warner accused me of spoiling their outings with girls but I didn't care. I quietly hugged to myself the delight of having proof that Sid had meant what he said. However, there was one girl I was a bit afraid of. She helped manage the cheese factory where Sid took milk twice a day, which meant he saw her many more times than me. She was very beautiful, with a lovely complexion and auburn hair. I knew she liked him something special and I was afraid that she would win Sid's affection, if my mother did not relent and allow us a little time together. So I plucked up my courage, determined to make a stand for something I wanted so badly. I had silently rehearsed what I was going to say to her and, the first evening we were alone, I gulped: "Mother, what have you got against Sid?" She answered: "I have nothing at all against him. He is the nicest boy in the village." I went on to explain about the girl working at the cheese dairy and with great daring I told mother that, if I lost Sid to this girl, I would blame her for ruining my life and would hold it against her while ever I lived. Quietly she replied: "If Sid loves you, he will wait for you until you are old enough." I cried myself to sleep that night for I thought mother so hard and implacable on this very special subject, although now I realize she was nothing of the kind.

A short while afterwards there was a dance in our new village hall, which had been built next door to our building yard, in fact on part of one of father's fields. Unfortunately, I had a bad cold and was not going to the dance, although by now I was mad on dancing. I was sadly watching my sister Florrie titivating in front of the mirror: she was wearing a pink dress with a pinafore front edged with marabou down and she looked divine. There I was sniffling away, tears running, supposedly reading an Ethel M. Dell novel, with the book upside down. I sat watching at the window, hoping I would see Sid on his way to the dance. I waved to him and, after he had gone by, I was biting my lips to stop myself crying when mother said to Florrie: "If Sid is at the dance, tell him he can come if he likes and sit with Nellie for a little while." I could have hugged her. Florrie had only been gone a few minutes when Sid came running to our door. Mother said to let him in, but by then I was halfway to the door. That night was bliss because, after that first invitation, my mother capitulated and our courtship was well and truly on its way. Sid stayed so long that night that mother said he had better go or he would miss all the dancing he had paid for. "Oh, I don't mind that, Mrs Wootton," he said, but he was reminded that Nellie had a bad cold and should soon be in bed.

My brother Warner and sister Florrie started going steady about this time as well. Warner met his future wife at a dance in Burton on the Wolds, a village two miles away, to which he had walked one warm night with several friends who wanted to see their new village hall. Among those from Barrow on Soar, a larger village the other side of Burton, was a fair-haired girl in a sleeveless green dress. Warner danced with her most of the evening and later he bought a motorcycle so he could continue his courting seriously. One night he ran into a cow that had strayed on to the road, but he was not seriously hurt. Father made enquiries about claiming damages from the cow's owner, but he found that the owner might then claim for damages to the cow.

Florrie had gone to Loughborough as a lady's companion, but she still cycled to Wymeswold to sing soprano solos in the church choir. The new organist and choirmaster, John Taylor, who was very strict with the choristers, also lived in Loughborough, and he started cycling to and fro with Florrie for choir practices and services in our church. Cycles thus played a key role in a second family courtship.

It was after church services and choir practices that Sid was first allowed to take me home, but I had to be back by 8-30. Gradually I was allowed an extension to 9-30 and, until I was married, I had to be in by that time when I was alone with Sid. The funny part was that, when we went to dances, in groups, we were allowed to stay out until three o'clock in the morning. Where the difference lay I could never fathom, for invariably we split up into twos on our way home.

By the time I was eighteen I was seeing more of Sid. In the winter I saw him on Sunday nights after church, Wednesday nights after choir practice and Saturday nights when we danced nearly every dance together. During the summer evenings we also enjoyed seeing each other at the tennis club. We saw each other so often my father one night teased me by looking over his glasses and saying: "Umm, you'll be wanting to live with him next." Greatly daring, I replied: "Yes, father, that's just what I hope to do one day."

During our courtship my dressmaking business was flourishing. I was so happy about this, as by this time we were both saving hard to get married at some future date. After a while Miss Simpson decided to visit her sister at Wisbech, so with a lot of 'dos and don'ts' she left me to manage the shop for five days. I enjoyed this work, using any spare moments to weigh out sugar, a half hundredweight at a time, and lard, currants and sultanas a stone at a time, into one-, two-, three- and four-pound bags, to try to keep the shelves well supplied. I did not do too badly and, when Miss Simpson came home, she was very pleased, for she had not had a holiday for years and had enjoyed the change and rest immensely.

Miss Simpson was a perfectionist in everything she did, keeping her shop in immaculate condition. She, like my mother, was a great believer in "a place for everything and everything in its place". She even knew when I had sold some wool from a certain box, because I had not put it back on the shelf in exactly the same way as she did herself. She was also a stern disciplinarian: children who came for sweets had to wipe their shoes and mothers were not allowed to sit their babies on the counter. I have heard her say: "Babies' bottoms should not be put where one puts one's food."

I could not help but notice that she never asked Sid to our house, yet John, my sister's boyfriend, was occasionally asked. It became increasingly clear that she was against me going out with Sid. I could not understand why and I dared not ask her but, the night before I was married, Aunt Becky put her arms around me and sobbed. She told me she would miss me, even more than my own mother would, as I had been like a daughter to her over the years of working and sleeping in her house. I was greatly moved by this emotion, as she had always been in such control of herself and I had never seen her cry before. After Sid and I were married, she changed her attitude entirely towards him and we were both welcomed into her home whenever we wished to go. Later she admitted she had not encouraged our courtship because she had not wanted to lose me. I promised her she would never lose me, even though I married, and that Sid would always help her in every way possible. This he proved as the years went by.

13 SID'S FAMILY

Sid's father, John Smith, was a much-respected Wymeswold gentleman. He had left school at the age of eleven years. He was the eldest of a family of five children whose parents had died before his teens within a period of two years. John Smith and his sister Lizzie were adopted by their Uncle John and Aunt Carolyn Smith, who were childless and lived at their farm on the corner of Wysall Lane, where future generations of Smiths were born and bred. Their sister Nan was adopted by a Mrs Moore, whose husband later became the Lord Mayor of London. The three youngest children were brought up in a home and were called Carrie, Lou and Sally. Sally died of meningitis when she was seventeen. Carrie married and lived in London. Lou married and lived in Bristol.

John was sent back to school for two years after he was adopted by his Uncle John. Lizzie became a schoolteacher: she taught all our family at the Wymeswold Church School. When my future father-in-law married, he left his uncle's farm and settled in a smallholding called Wisteria Farm at the east end of the village. There they worked terribly hard making up the milk from a small herd of cattle into Stilton cheese. They had to borrow ten pounds from sister Lizzie, who was teaching at the time, to tide them over while their Stiltons matured and were ready for sale. To help financially, they took in a schoolteacher lodger named Miss Dulake, who became a life-long friend of the Smith family. Sid was born at Wisteria Farm and, when he was eight years old, they all moved back to the family farm at Wysall Lane End. John's Aunt Carolyn had passed away, leaving Uncle John with only Lizzie. There they all farmed until the time came when Sid and I, with our two small sons, took over. Sid's father then farmed around seventy acres, mostly grass, with a milking herd of around seventeen cows and their followers, calves

and yearlings. Sid was his father's only regular helper on the farm but casual help was hired at harvest and haymaking times.

Sid's mother was a beautiful woman with a great sense of humour; she could mimic most people perfectly. Her name was Lizzie Mitchell and her parents kept the Three Crowns Inn in the village. Lizzie's father reared and trained hunters. In her youth she rode these horses in the home field to show off their paces. When the gentleman buyers came to see the horses, they usually had dinner at their home, and Lizzie would help her mother to prepare these very special meals for the hunting gentlemen. This knowledge proved useful when her mother became ill and one of those special dinners had been ordered. Lizzie used to tell how, at the age of thirteen, she prepared, cooked and served a chicken dinner with all the accompanying dishes. She was warmly congratulated by the gentlemen and given a substantial tip. Lizzie had one sister who married an architect and she lived in West Bridgford near Nottingham for many years, later moving to a village called Knowle just outside Birmingham.

Being a dressmaker, I was interested to hear my mother-in-law's opinion that the best-dressed woman was the one who dressed for the occasion. She herself was certainly one of the best-dressed women I knew. She always bought very good clothes which lasted a long time, since she chose clothes that did not date quickly.

One could sit for hours listening to her stories. I loved to hear the ones about her youth, especially those about Sid when he was a small boy. Once, when he was three years old, Sid went with his father into the garden to weed between the kidney bean plants. When his father finished the row, he straightened his back and turned round to look at his handiwork, only to find that his young son had helped by pulling up every bean plant. What a lengthy job it was to reset the plants. Another memory was when Sid was five years old. He came in from play, looking guilty and saying he was very poorly. His mother sat him comfortably in a chair and then went out into the yard to see if she could discover what was wrong. There she found a young cockerel lying as though it was dead. She picked it up and the cockerel suddenly recovered, and she let it strut away. Sid meanwhile had followed his mother and had seen the cockerel hopping away. "Oh! oh!" he said. "It's got up again. I thought it was dead when I hit it on its head. I feel better now it's up again."

Outside the house of Perry Hardy, my grandfather's second wife, Sid and a friend named Cyril Hubbard, who was a couple of years younger than Sid, were playing dangerously underneath a tethered horse. Perry told them quite sharply to go home. This they pretended to do but, on looking out of her window, Perry saw they were there again. She told them she would report them both to their parents but was amused by Sid's answer. He looked at her and said: "I wish, I wish Cyril Hubbard would call you a silly old fool." These two boys were again into mischief when they sat astride a pig which was close to farrowing. They sat back to back, one holding the pig's ears, the other holding its tail. They raced this poor pig until it literally dropped with exhaustion. They really did get into trouble for this escapade, but the pig recovered and delivered her litter without mishap.

Another amusing story was when an old village character named Peter, who occasionally helped out at busy times on the farm, became very inquisitive when he smelt cooking coming from the farmhouse kitchen. Many times he had popped his head through the window saying: "Lizzie, gis us a taste." One day he asked: "What's cooking, Lizzie?" "Strawberry jam," was the answer. "Want a taste, Peter?" "Sure do," says Peter, opening his mouth wide. In popped a huge spoonful of very hot chutney. "Blast yer eyes," says Peter, "you've bunt me mouth out."

Another cooking story was when my brother Warner, who was around eight years old at the time, was given a couple of mince pies made by Sid's mother. Miss Dulake, who was living at the farm, said: "Warner, your mam can't make mince pies as good as these, can she?" Warner said: "Yes, she can, a lot better than hers." But when Warner told our mam this story, he said: "Mam, Mrs Smith can make mince pies a lot better than yours, but I wasn't going to tell her that."

Sid had a sister named Kathleen and a younger brother, Bob. When Kathleen was a baby, her auntie took her into the Post Office where Mrs Brown, the postmistress, was holding her baby Connie. A customer started to admire the baby Kathleen, remarking what a bonnie baby she was. Mrs Brown felt a bit slighted, as nothing was said about her baby, so she informed everyone in the shop that her baby was "quality not quantity". Not to be outdone, Kathleen's auntie drew herself up and said quietly: "This baby is quality and quantity."

Another of Sid's mother's stories concerned a gentleman farmer, one of the village's notable residents, who drove a pony and gig. He was once three miles away from the village, when he passed a young farm labourer walking home from work. The gentleman stopped his horse and asked the young man if he would like a lift into the village. The lad answered: "I don't mind if I do." The gentleman replied: "If you don't mind, I'm sure I don't." And with that remark he whipped up his horse and drove on. The youth wondered what he had done wrong, for the words "I don't mind if I do" were generally used to mean "Yes".

A friend of Sid's mother played a trick on her husband one extremely cold night. The friend's husband had shuddered at the thought of getting into his cold bed and his wife had said: "Oh, off you go. I'll bring the warming pan as soon as I've filled it with warm coals." He was looking forward to his bed being warmed, so when his wife brought up the warming pan, he tucked his legs up under his body to enable his better half to warm the lower half of the bed. Suddenly she brought up the warming pan straight on to his buttocks. The husband screamed out: "You bugger, you've bunt me bum." The laughable part was that his wife had filled the warming pan with hard frosted snow.

14 EARLY MARRIAGE YEARS

Between the two great wars was the time of marriage within our family. Warner, Florrie and I were all married within the space of one year and it was my delight to make most of the wedding dresses. My own wedding dress was a light-beige georgette material with lace trimmings. The bridesmaids were my sister Edna and Sid's sister Kathleen and they wore dresses in pale-pink georgette. My bouquet was unique, for it was made with very special roses. The florist persuaded me to have it made with a new, expensive but very beautiful rose, which had only recently been placed on the market. She said: "Please have it, Miss Wootton, for it will be the first bouquet that I will have made using this rose." I wanted to have this glorious rose but, because we were both cost-conscious in practically everything we did, I looked questioningly at Sid, for he was paying the bill. His answer was that, as we were only going to be married once, I was to have it.

This rose was a new variety from Holland. The growers, not wanting it to be taken by the invading Germans during the First World War, had shipped it to America for safety. When peace was declared, they decided that the only possible name for this beautiful rose was "Peace".

When Warner and Sybil were married, she wore a pinky-beige georgette dress made by her friend. Her bridesmaids were her sister Edith and our sister Florrie who wore blue dresses. When Florrie was married, she wore this dress for her going-away outfit. Warner and Sybil started their married life in a small derelict bakehouse, owned by mother, which Warner converted into quite a nice cottage. It had a large living room with a kitchen recess, a sitting room, one large and one small bedroom and the usual washhouse outside across the yard.

Florrie and John were next to be married. Her dress was ivory georgette and had a fashionable pinafore front. Our sisters Lottie and Edna and two small cousins of John were bridesmaids. Lottie and Edna wore pale-green georgette and the tiny girls wore ivory silk dresses. Florrie and John started their married life in a furnished house just opposite where our family used to live in Clay Street. The rent was ten shillings per week, which was considered a very high rent, but even in those days accommodation was very hard to find. Shortly after they were married, John fell out of work, one of many who, during those deep depressions of the thirties, joined the dole queue. He was paid 27/6d per week. It was a sad blow for John and Florrie, for their only other income was John's organist's pay. John hated being out of work and after a while they obtained a caretaker's job at a large house between Swithland and Woodhouse Eaves. This job kept body and soul together until John returned to his work as an inspector of lifts and cranes.

When Sid and I were married, we had been promised a cottage in Brook Street which was owned by Dr Tawse, an ear, nose and throat specialist at Nottingham Hospital who lived at Wymeswold Hall. At that time it was occupied by a lady who had been recently widowed, and we were allowed to have it on condition that we waited until the lady moved out, which Dr Tawse thought would be about three weeks. However, the waiting period lengthened into many months, so Sid and I started our married life in two rooms in his parents' farmhouse. These months were very happy indeed. I became very close to Kathleen, my sister-in-law, during that time and a friendship was formed that has held fast over fifty years of close contact through both happy and extremely sad times.

Our first son, John Sidney, was born at my mother's house one Saturday. I suffered a very hard time during this first birth which was an extended breech. The baby was in a bad way, but Dr Bostock gave him the kiss of life and after a while he came round and was a sound healthy baby. Mother was much disturbed at the hard time I was having. Seeing her so upset distressed me, so I asked her to leave the doctor and me to it. The family was all waiting downstairs along with Sid. The doctor told mother to send Sid and everyone out for a walk, as it would be some time before the baby arrived. Mother thought she had sent them all safely away, including Sid, and looking through the bedroom window, she saw them walking up the lane. Suddenly, under the bedroom window, we heard a slight cough and there was my beloved Sid who had doubled back over the field to be near if he was needed. It was not considered proper in those days for the father to be present when his wife gave birth, but Sid had stayed with me until the very last moment when the nurse had turned him out. However, he was upstairs again as soon as he was allowed. I was sitting up in bed, cuddling our son, when Sid came in. I remember him entering the room on tiptoe looking so awed at becoming a father.

Sid was nervous of holding the baby. "He is so little," he said. "Little be hanged," I exclaimed. "Our baby is a bouncing nine pounds two ounces." Sid thought the baby looked just like himself and I told him those were the exact words that Dr Bostock had used: "He's like old Sid."

Dr Bostock was the family doctor to both Sid's family and mine and we all loved him. When he first came to Wymeswold, he travelled round the villages in a high dog cart pulled by a beautiful horse, which stood quietly outside the surgery until all the patients had gone. Then the doctor would trot his horse round the streets visiting the bedridden patients. After a few years he bought a motor cycle which caused great excitement, and later on a two-seater motor car which he ran for years.

Meanwhile, our cottage had become vacant and, after the birth of Sidney junior, we moved in and there we spent an unbelievably happy four years. As I was recovering from the birth of Sidney, Lottie helped me prepare our cottage. It had three bedrooms, two front rooms, a large living-kitchen and a larder down two steps. Mother looked after the baby while we scrubbed out the kitchen, staircase and larder.

The next day Sid and I went to Loughborough with as much money as we could spare and all our wedding-present money that we had saved to help furnish our home. To future generations who set up home and think what a lot it costs, compare the prices we paid. We bought a new lino for our bedroom at 4/6d a square yard, a new bedstead and mattress for seven pounds, a second-hand bedroom suite in walnut for eleven pounds and three bedside mats for 12/6d each. Then we bought the baby a new cot and mattress for 47/6d. A dinner-set cost four pounds.

In my excitement at buying so many things, I had done a dreadful thing, for I discovered I had left my handbag somewhere on the way through the shop. All the money we had saved, including our wedding present money, was in that bag. I was frantically rushing from floor to floor, asking if any of the assistants had seen it. When we reached the department on the bottom floor, where we had bought a pram for five pounds, there, much to our relief, was my bag sitting on the counter where I had so carelessly left it. The gentleman behind the counter provided me with a chair and asked me to sit down, as I had received a nasty shock. (This man was not to know – and for that matter neither did we – that eighteen years later he would sell Sid and me a twin pram.)

I was very proud of our bedroom. The walls had been papered in pale blue and the paintwork was white. Mother had given me all the linen, blankets and an eiderdown. For our living-kitchen we bought only two new things: a strip of lino to put across the middle of the brick floor and four new dining chairs. We were given an armchair and sofa to match and we had purchased one new bed-chair while living at the farm. We used my old dressmaking table and, a couple of years before we were married, I had bought at a sale an antique oak chest of drawers which served as a sideboard all the time we lived at the cottage. This oak chest of drawers is now worth more than eight times the cost of our first home. To enable me to sew, we did buy a good oil lamp.

Sid's father told him he would retire in a few years, if we could pay for all the cattle and implements on entering the family farm, so Sid thought we could not spend any more on our little cottage but should start to save for the farm. I did so want to furnish our sitting-room, so after we had settled into the two rooms, I started to take in dressmaking again. With the money I saved, I hoped to buy a lino and a three-piece suite. I found it quite impossible to save anything from Sid's wages, as he earned only two pounds per week. I put away ten shillings for rent and 1/6d per week for rates and this money was never touched until it was rent day once a quarter. The remaining 28/6d was used for all other needs. It was quite a struggle to make ends meet, but I enjoyed every moment, economizing in every way I could. If my grocery bill came to more than 7/6d, I had to cross something off the list, usually a small tin of Sid's favourite pineapple which cost only fourpence halfpenny. Butter cost 8d a pound, as did cheese. Bread was fourpence a large loaf, tea 6d per quarter, sugar twopence halfpenny a pound, as was a pint of milk. A joint out of the middle of a leg of lamb was two shillings and sixpence and a piece of top side of beef cost one shilling and twopence per pound. Beef sausage one could buy for 6d a pound and pork sausage for 8d. Our coal was 1/3d a hundredweight.

Sid went to work at six o'clock in the morning and had one hour off for his dinner, unless he was ploughing, when he would take bread and cheese and have his dinner at four o'clock, to be ready for milking at five. In the summer, when haymaking or gathering in the harvest, he would not be home until dark hour. Despite the long summer working hours, Sid did not receive any extra wages. Until we were married, Sid never had a wage, for farmer's sons in those days did not expect one. Sid earned his pocket money by doing a little contract work with his father's horses and carts when he had finished on his father's farm. He also had a breeding pig and a hut with forty or fifty laying hens. A calf was given to him for a wedding present which he reared along with his father's calves, but when the calf grew up and produced a calf itself, Sid's father had the milk, apart from what we needed for our own use. Perhaps this seemed a bit hard, but in return Sid had a calf each year that grazed on his father's field, a pig which raised two litters each year which he sold, and a small income from eggs, for Sid was a wizard at making hens lay well. The profit from these animals and birds was put away in Sid's bank in readiness for the time when we took over the farm. We used some of that money only once, when for my twenty-seventh birthday Sid bought me a brand-new piano which cost forty-two guineas. Sid's father, who was not musical at all, was much displeased at Sid spending so much on a piano, for he said Sid could have bought two good heifers for that price. However, Sid's mother was delighted when she saw my fine new piano and she told father-in-law that Nellie worked extremely hard, had missed not having a piano to play and deserved this one luxury. Sid's father came round in the end, as he always did if mother-in-law was in favour.

My baby became an increasing delight to me. He was a child who needed a tremendous amount of sleep, which was a great help to me, as I was completing an almost full-time job with my dressmaking. Sid and I were very happy in our new home. Neither of us felt any need to go out; we were quite content to stay at home improving the house and garden.

The garden was quite large and we grew all our own vegetables. We also had a sizeable orchard with all kinds of fruit, most of which I bottled or preserved. At the bottom of our garden was a herb bed with mint, parsley and what I thought was sage. One day Sid brought me a rabbit and asked if I could cook it the way his mother did, as she was a splendid cook who always made this particular dish taste delicious. To make sure I had all the ingredients for the stuffing, I tripped down to the farm to ask her. I counted all the ingredients on my fingers and rushed back home to prepare the rabbit. One had to boil it gently until tender, then add this concoction and simmer for about twenty minutes. I was delighted with the result: the dish looked very appetizing, exactly the way Sid's mother cooked it. I placed Sid's dinner in front of him and I watched him start to eat. A look of distaste came over his face and

I tried mine. Oh dear, it tasted terrible. Sid tried another mouthful, then pushed his plate away, saying: "It looks alright, Nell, but I can't eat it. What have you put in the stuffing?" I counted once again on my fingers all the things I had used, ending with sage. "Where did you get the sage from?" asked Sid. He asked me to show him just where I had picked it. We walked up the garden with our arms round each other and I showed Sid the place. He turned me round to face him, shook me soundly and laughed: "You're priceless, Nell. That is a lavender bed." We raced each other back to the house and tucked into a lunch of bread and cheese with pickles, filling up with rice pudding. I was teased unmercifully for many months as my lavender stuffing story became known. Sid's leg was pulled by his farmer friends when he went to market.

Our baby had just started to walk when Sid went into hospital for a nose operation. He had to have a bone chipped away, because he could breathe through only one nostril. This overgrowth of bone was caused through an accident he had suffered while out riding. The horse put its foot in a rabbit hole when they were galloping round the field. The horse was brought down, falling on Sid and damaging his nose. He endured the discomfort for several years, before he mentioned it to our landlord, Dr Tawse, who used to come round on Sunday mornings to chat with Sid. Dr Tawse kindly told Sid to visit him at his nursing home so he could look at it, and his wife would drive him into Nottingham the next time she went into town. Arrangements were made with Mrs Tawse, who was one of the few ladies who drove a motor car, and Sid was told he had to have a few pieces chipped from the bone to allow him to breathe through both nostrils. He was admitted to Nottingham General Hospital where the operation was performed, and he was kept in for ten days. The day before he was due to be discharged, he developed a sore throat which made it hard to swallow. He refused his food but did not say anything to the nurses for fear of being kept in the hospital for a longer period. When he arrived home, he had a fever and felt extremely ill. It was obvious he had caught something serious during his stay in hospital. However, nothing was diagnozed but, when the baby also became ill, I sent for Dr Bostock who said he had scarlet fever. Sid's sister Kathleen and my brother Billie had both spent a day with us and had been in close contact with the baby. I had even found baby Sidney and Billie chewing gum from mouth to mouth to see how far it could be stretched before it broke in the middle. Kathleen and Billie both caught scarlet fever and we were all quite sure the illness had started with Sid's visit to the hospital. Both Kathleen and Billie were confined for six weeks in a room on their own. I did not catch it, because I had had scarlet fever with the rest of the family before the time of Billie's birth, so I was one of the few allowed to visit them.

Sid decided to buy an incubator to hatch out our own chicks. This we put in our unused downstairs room. We did so well with this incubator that we bought another one, selling the day-old chicks to other farmers. Using eggs from our own hens, we set one hundred and fifty eggs in each incubator. We usually attained an eighty per cent average of live chicks. We both loved this part of our work and we spent much time watching the chicks through the window of the incubator fighting their way out of their shells. First one could hear a tapping noise, then a tiny hole would appear, always in the same place in the shell, and after a few moments a tiny beak would be seen. The chicks then seemed to rest a while, then the pecking would start again until the whole head peeped out. After another rest there would be a tremendous effort which broke the shell in half, and a wet, tired little chick would flop down among the others. Some, of course, never made it, poor little things, for they would die because they were not strong enough to fight their way out. The specialist hatchers maintain that a chick not strong enough to hatch on its own would never be any good and would die later. It was a great temptation to help a chick out that was having difficulty but, if the incubator door was opened, the moisture would escape and all the chicks would be in trouble. We did this once to our regret, since we lost many of our good chicks when the fresh air got inside the incubator and dried the moisture which enables them to struggle from their shells. Sid bought a good sound hen house at a farm sale, installed it in our orchard and filled it with about thirty pullets. These paid a good dividend which we put into the bank to help swell the farm fund.

An interesting experiment took place with one of these pullets that became broody. She was a white hen with brown speckles, called Clara. Sid sat her on fourteen eggs which hatched out three weeks later, but Sid took away the chicks, giving them to another broody hen. Then he put another fourteen eggs under Clara, who in another three weeks hatched a further batch of healthy chicks. Sid considered repeating the process, but I thought it would be cruel to poor old Clara, so she was allowed to keep her babies. Afterwards, when she had finished rearing her chicks, she laid one egg for thirty-one consecutive days. Good going, that:

Our baby was now growing into a sturdy two-year old and was always into mischief. One day I thought he was very quiet when he should have been playing on the lawn. I went outside to investigate and found him in one of the outhouses, where he had half emptied a hundredweight bag of poultry meal and mixed it with soil. He was busily mixing it the way he had seen Grandpa Wootton do with sand and cement. I was cross with him and told him he must not do that again, but a few days later there he was again, doing the same thing but on another bag. When his father chastised him, little Sidney said: ""I didn't touch the bag you told me not to. I did this one."

Around this time Kathleen went to college for three years. Father-in-law told me that it would cost three pounds per week to send Kathleen, for at that time parents had to pay the expenses of their young ones if they attended college. Kathleen was a true home girl and, although she was keen to attend college, she was affected greatly at leaving her home in the country for the life of Goldsmiths College in London. Fortunately, she had her two aunties, her father's sisters, living in London not far away from her college, who always had their homes open to welcome Kathleen and her friends. Although I was happy for Kathleen to go to college, I knew I was going to miss her very much, for we had become very close since my marriage to Sid and she was wonderful with young Sidney who was then three years old. He idolised her and was really upset when he was told his beloved aunt was going away. Kathleen and I both remember just what he said: "Don't on't you go to tollege, Auntie Kath. I vill tum to tollege, and my shall say: 'Tum on out of tollege, Auntie Kath.' Dat vot my vill say."

By this time I thought I had better count the money I had made from dressmaking. It amounted to nearly thirty pounds, so we made enquiries as to how much a three-piece suite would cost. After much discussion we decided to ask a man who had recently set up on his own in this line of business to give us an estimate and patterns of different quality moquette. Needless to say, I chose the best which was to cost twenty-five pounds. We never regretted choosing the top price, for this moquette lasted nearly thirty years of real hard wear with a growing family. The colours of the suite were deep wine and black on a silver grey background. After paying for it, I still had enough money left to buy some new lino to cover the old brick floor.

Only a few months after we had furnished our sitting room, we suffered torrential rain day after day. After three days the brook in our street burst its banks. The whole street was flooded, including the paths on each side. We watched anxiously as the houses opposite became flooded with the swirling water. Fortunately, our house was raised, having two stone steps up to the front door. As darkness drew near, the water had only half an inch to rise before it entered our house and we thought that our treasured piano and furniture would have to be carried upstairs. Sid put on his outdoor clothes and prepared to get help quickly. As he went out by the front door, he looked at the water rushing down the street and tried to calculate how much longer it would be before our cottage was flooded, but after a few minutes he said: "Look, Nell. I believe the flood is going down." Sure enough, I noticed a faint line where the water had reached and, as we waited, we could see that the water was receding, oh so slowly but surely. We were much relieved at last to see a one-inch tidemark gradually becoming greater and the relentless rain had stopped. However, we sat up well into the night

before we assured ourselves that it would be safe to go to bed. In the morning the flood was well down, the bridges across the brook became usable again and the people opposite received help with their mopping-up operations. We were thankful to have escaped by such a narrow margin.

Soon after the great flood, I became pregnant with my second child. It was not an easy pregnancy and I often felt quite unwell. Towards the end of that time Auntie Becky suffered a thrombosis, so I kept her shop open for six weeks and looked after her in the daytime, sister Lottie doing night duty. I went home that last Saturday night unutterably weary. On Sunday I cooked our dinner and on Monday I cleaned our cottage right through, taking particular care in our bedroom, changing the sheets in readiness for my confinement which by now I knew was near. When Sid came home for his dinner, I asked him to stay home with me as my pains were strong and quite frequent. He became all hot and bothered and said: "I'm going to fetch me mum." When she arrived, she soon organized things. She sent Sid on his cycle to fetch the district nurse, prepared a bath for me and helped me into bed. When the nurse arrived, she made a pot of tea, but secretly I knew there would be no time to drink it as the baby was coming. The nurse just had time to take off her coat and wash before our second son was born. Now, silly like, I had never thought our second baby would be a boy, and I had made all the layette in pink, certain we would have a girl. When Grandma Smith said it was a boy, the nurse said: "Shush, I haven't looked yet." "Ah," said grandma, "but I've seen." This was the first baby she had seen born and our new little son, to be called David, was her favourite all her life. I thought he was ugly, not at all like baby Sidney who had been a good-looker from birth. When Sid saw him, he thought: "We have a right ugly duckling here." The baby was red-faced, with a head that came up to a point, but within a week he lost all these features and had become a most beautiful baby.

During the time we lived at the cottage, a few days before her twenty-first birthday, my sister Edna was involved in a serious accident. She had gone on a bus to visit an auntie living in

Loughborough. On alighting at her destination, instead of waiting for the bus to depart, she tripped round to the front of the bus and, in crossing the road, was picked up on to the bonnet of a passing car travelling at a normal speed. The car carried her many yards, then threw her off and, it was thought, ran over her. My sister was taken unconscious to Loughborough Hospital with little hope of recovery. Needless to say, our family was in a dreadful state, but mother, with her usual calm, helped everyone to bear the anxiety of the days of Edna's coma. Only mother was allowed to visit her. The rest of the family had to wait for better news, but day after day there was no change in her condition. Mother told us that Edna's body was literally black and blue all over with bruises. She also had an awful leg wound but it was her head that everyone was most worried about. Edna was unconscious on her twenty-first birthday, but after around a week there was a miracle, for she regained consciousness. The family knew by my mother's face when she returned home that day that she would tell us better news.

During Edna's convalescence she was so impressed by the dedication of the nurses at the hospital that she decided never to go back to her own work again but to train to be a nurse. She trained in Nottingham, passed her exams and became a state registered nurse. Later she became a sister, ending her career in London where she is now living in retirement.

15 THE FARM

We had been living at the cottage for three and a half years when father and mother-in-law decided to retire, so we started to prepare ourselves for the great adventure of becoming tenants at the family farm, where we would be the third generation of Smiths.

We moved in one Good Friday, when our second child was one year and four months old. Mother looked after the boys while we moved, which was a great help. We moved all our furniture with a horse and father's dray, which took two days. In my youth families moved their own furniture, unless they were leaving to live miles away. At first I missed our cottage with its many happy memories. Now we faced a massive task and we knew it would be done only gradually because of lack of money. The cattle, that is the live and dead farm stock as they are called at farm sales, had all been valued, and we had scraped the bottom of both our barrels to pay every penny. Grandpa Smith did not charge us any tenant right, as Sid had worked for him without a regular wage until we married.

All profits were ploughed back into the farm. I realized that any improvements in the farmhouse would be up to me, so I kept on my sewing, earning as much as I could. The farmhouse had three large living-rooms, two in the front and one at the side from which three steps led down into two large cellars where cheese used to be made. The slate vats and huge cheese press were still there and brick thralls surrounded all the walls. Since cheese making finished, the cellars were used as pantries.

There was still no piped water in the village and all the water, both for man and beast, was pumped out of the deep well just outside our back door. Sometimes in the summer the well would run dry when all the cattle had taken their fill, but after a few hours the spring which fed the well would refill it sufficiently to obtain enough water for house requirements. Only during a few very dry times did we have to fill the churns at the village pump in the Stockwell. There we had to take our turn in the queue of farmers' carts waiting for water to take to their animals. This pump was fed by a spring which had been known to dry up only once. When this happened, the farmers had to make a journey of two miles to the neighbouring village of Burton on the Wolds, where there was a spring which had never been known to run dry. It was called the 'Lion's Mouth' because the water ran through an effigy of a lion's head. The time came when our water supply became tainted. An inspector came to test the water, after which he condemned it for human consumption. Apparently the effluent from our huge muck heap was seeping into the spring which supplied the well and, even when the heap was cleared away and the earth base was replaced by a concrete foundation, it would be a long time before the water was fit for human consumption. As a result I had to carry two buckets full of water from a neighbour's farm or from the Stockwell pump for drinking purposes.

We knew that a lot of work was needed to make the farmhouse as we would like it. Electricity had recently come to the village, so we asked our landlords (Trinity College, Cambridge) if they would install this for us. The college was willing and a firm from Nottingham soon set about the job of bringing electric light to our farm. This work left every room in the house in need of decorating, so I earned the money by dressmaking and then I bought the paint and paper. Sid would not allow me to paper the ceilings, so I got a man to come and paper all the bedroom ceilings. Then I systematically papered every room in the house, starting upstairs where my papering would not be seen so often. When I eventually progressed downstairs I had become quite professional.

Of course, we did not go through all this decorating without some amusing incidents and some mishaps. One of these happened when I was papering the boys' room. It was the fashion at that time to put above the picture rail a frieze of paper the same as that on the ceiling. I had covered three parts of one wall, when I found I was stuck on the ladder with the length of paper in my hands and could not reach far enough to finish that piece. I yelled to Sid to come to my aid, which he promptly did, and I asked him to climb to where I was and to hold the paper while I climbed on to the other stepladder. I took the paper from Sid and, to my horror, found that both his hands had gone right through the paper and ruined it. All my painstaking work had to be pulled off and done all over again. To make matters worse, Sid started to tease me, tickling me so that I nearly fell off the stepladder. I finished up by throwing the brush at him, which of course he successfully ducked.

On another occasion I went to peep at the front hall ceiling paper, which had just been put on, only to find the whole lot had peeled away and was hanging down like a balloon. I called to Sid to come and look. He was in bed, so he came in his night shirt and stood at the top of the staircase, while I was downstairs looking up. Being Sid, he turned this catastrophe into a humorous situation by starting to do a ballet dance along the plank the paper-hanger had left, then he did the can-can, using his nightshirt flap to execute the flipping of the dress. One can imagine the one standing below seeing more than one should at every flip of the shirt flap. My sides ached and ached with laughter.

The far sitting room, which was used as an incubator room, was papered with a cheap paper costing fivepence halfpenny a ten-yard roll. Before we could start the other front sitting room, we had the unenviable job of peeling around seven old papers off the walls. We soaked and soaked these old papers, using first cold water, then hot, but they would not release their hold on the walls. One of the papers was a deep red colour and the dye ran out and mixed with the slosh on the floor. I worked at this horrible job every available moment for days without making much progress. One evening when I was completely worn out, Sid came in and exclaimed: "What a bloody mess, Nell!" Sid never swore, at least not in front of ladies, but what he said was literally true: the room looked like a slaughterhouse. Sid had a go at this obstinate paper, but after a few minutes he put down the scraper and walked out. "Uiuiu," I thought in a tired way, "Sid's soon had enough." But no, back he

came with a sharp spade in his hands, with which he tackled the walls once again. I left him to get on with the job, while I cleaned myself up and prepared supper. When I was ready, I went back into the room and Sid was brushing the bloody-looking wet mess into the hall and out of the front door to be loaded on to a cart and taken to the rubbish tip. Never was I so glad to see the back of such a repulsive heap, but worse was to come, for as I turned back to look at the walls, I realized with horror that the heavy-handed spadework had chipped huge pieces of plaster out of the walls, necessitating complete new plaster on every wall. I realized later that this was to the good really, as the old plaster was crumbling all over the place. My father saw to this work and after a while, when the plaster had dried out (for plaster did not contain the drying element it has today), we could at long last start to decorate our best room.

The paper we chose was a thickly embossed beige colour. Before covering the old brick floor with lino, we filled in the deep cracks with bran. Then we finished off with a carpet square which cost four pounds, nineteen shillings and sixpence. The room looked beautiful, so we moved the piano and our three-piece suite into position, then went to bed, tired but content. Every friend that came to see us had to be shown our newly-decorated sitting-room. But pride took a bad tumble for, as time went on, I could detect a mouldy smell which gradually became a mouldy stink. Then I noticed the lino bulging all over the floor. The penny dropped: the bran I had used to fill up the cracks between the bricks had become damp, causing it to swell and smell. How stupid can a young wife be! I certainly ought to have had more sense. The room had to be cleared, the carpet and lino taken up, the floor scrubbed with disinfectant and left a couple of weeks to sweeten and dry out. The next time I used a fine sand for filling and everything was right at last with our sitting-room.

To furnish and equip our house, we bought a lot of things at sales. In Loughborough a young couple were selling up their home to start a new life abroad. We bought from them a zinc bath which we filled with other stuff we had bought: saucepans, kettles, colanders, in fact nearly everything one needs in a kitchen for cooking. We strapped everything we could to our bicycles. Sid hung things around his neck and he carried the overfull bath under one arm, riding one-handed. I was similarly loaded and had to ride one-handed, too. We caused a stir in Loughborough as we clinked and clanked our way home. People waved and shouted laughable slogans after us, but we didn't care one little bit, we were so happy with our day's outing and all the good bargains we had bought.

By the time our house had been put in reasonable order, the haymaking season had arrived. Grandpa Smith had always shared the haymaking equipment with a friend of his named Harry Tyler, but this meant that the two of them were making hay for weeks on end and in a catchy rainy season a lot of hay was often lost. Sid and I discussed this matter from all angles. I was all for launching out on our own with a new mowing-machine, dividing the other machines and buying the rest we needed. Sid was dubious, however, for he thought Mr Tyler would be hurt at breaking up the long partnership, but I had no qualms, as I knew I was not one of Mr Tyler's favourite people and was not really welcomed into the partnership. Sid then made the excuse that we hadn't enough money to buy a new mowing machine, let alone a rake and other equipment. I surprised him by saying that I had saved enough with my dressmaking to buy one and that clinched it. We bought the new machine at a cost of twenty-seven pounds, which left me with only two pounds in my Post Office account, but I was well satisfied. That first year my father lent us some of his equipment and our haymaking was finished in record time, every hand working full out. My brother Warner helped us in the evenings along with other friends of Sid. Grandpa Smith was a tremendous help during all our busy times and his advice was sought and appreciated. Sid was delighted at the speed with which we cleared our fields, without the interruption of taking turns with Mr Tyler's fields.

Our first harvest was one of the best we ever had, yielding a heavy weight of grain per acre. We always said that first splendid harvest put us on our feet. A bad harvest could have put us back years.

Sid's brother Bob stayed with us and helped on the farm as he had helped his father.

On a farm where animals are kept there is always the risk of a slight percentage in losses one way or another. One can give a big price for a young heifer, only to find that she proves to be a poor milker and has to be fattened up for meat. A dreaded disease in a milking herd was mastitis which could work havoc with a good cow's udder, but nowadays science has cleared away many of these troubles.

We took another great risk when we bought a horse from a neighbouring farmer. Not having enough work to do, it had become a loss to this gentle farmer. Sid and his brother Bob were both fine horsemen, but this was one of two horses that beat them good and proper. It was a terribly excitable animal and resented all efforts to control him, but eventually Sid and Bob had a measure of success with only the occasional lapse, such as the day when Bob took the horse on a five mile journey to fetch a load of timber. Everything went well until he came to a steep hill. The horse was halfway up with his heavy load when he decided he could not make it. Then the fun started, for he reared and stamped, getting more and more excited every moment. Bob decided to unload half the timber to see if the horse would manage that amount. He tackled the horse to the dray again and he sailed away to the top of the hill. Then, of course, the half-load on the dray had to be taken off and put on the grass at the side of the road, and back they went down the hill to pick up the other half. When the horse and dray were back at the top of the hill, Bob had to load up again the timber lying at the side of the road. We were getting quite worried at the length of time young Bob was away on this journey and were much relieved when we saw him drive safely into the yard.

On another occasion this horse thought he could not do a job he was set to do in one of the fields. Sid was driving him when he started his antics. He became so excited, stamping and threshing about, that his nose began to bleed. My goodness, I never saw anything like it, for the blood poured out like water from a pump. We sent for the vet who plugged his nose with lots of cotton wool, which eventually stopped the bleeding. To our surprise, the vet said the horse could be worked normally after a few days.

Mr Phillips, the vet, had attended my father's animals but did not remember me as the little Miss Wootton he used to know, for I had grown in my late teens to a normal height, He looked just the same to me as he looked all those years ago, a perfect English gentleman – or so I thought until one day when he was called to one of our sick cows. Not knowing at what time the vet would call, Sid left me explanations about the cow's symptoms. On examination of the cow, Mr Phillips asked for a whisky bottle to drench the cow. When I fetched him the bottle, along with some warm water, he looked at the bottle, furiously turned to me and shouted: "I don't want that bugger, but one with a long neck." I realized then the kind he needed and hastened to fetch one. After he had drenched the cow, a very difficult job on one's own, washed his hands, put on his coat and was preparing to leave, I looked straight at him, thanked him for giving the cow the much-needed medicine while my husband was away, and then told him that I was surprised that a gentleman of his standing should use such obscene language to a lady who had not deserved it, having fetched just what he had asked for. In subsequent meetings with the vet, I knew he held no grudge against me for my sharp reprimand. In fact, he was nicer to me than he had ever been before. In later years Mr Phillips was talking to my brother John who happened to mention my name and that I was his sister. He told John that never had anyone made him feel so small or had stuck up to him when he was in a violent temper as I had. He smiled at John and said he had admired me ever since. In my young days we were taught to respect the vet, the same as the doctor and the vicar, and my retaliation to his bad behaviour would have been considered highly out of place.

During a very severe winter I took a short walk to watch Sid digging out a posthole to hang a field gate. Although the weather was bitterly cold, Sid was sweating at the exertion of digging three feet down into the frozen earth, having to use a pick to loosen the soil. This job, which should have taken less than an hour, took over half the day, but it had to be finished, as the gate led to the highway and the cattle were let out into the field for exercise, even though the weather was so severe. The post Sid was using was a heavy oak one made from beams taken out of the church belfry where the bells were being rehung. Although these posts were removed because of woodworm, that post is still there forty years after, as good as it ever was.

At that time, after weeks and weeks of frost, Sid had to give up ploughing, as the horses were steaming with their exertions trying to pull the plough, It was unforgettable the sight of those horses as they walked into the yard. Although their bodies were steaming, icicles hung from their noses at least a foot long. Sid led them into the stable, rubbed them down, covered them with horse-cloths, fed them warm mash and gave them warm water to drink. How animals survived that winter I do not know. The frost was so severe that the urine in the chamber pots under the bed was frozen in the morning. Another sight only seen once was when rain beat on the sides of the houses and froze as it settled. Everything was coated with ice, looking as though it was encased in glass.

During another very hard frost there was an incident I remember with pride. Sid was ill with influenza and I had been in bed only a few minutes, enjoying our usual little chat before going to sleep, when we both heard distinctly the bellow of a cow in pain. Sid thought for a bit and then said that he didn't think the next cow was due for calving for at least another fortnight. We listened intently and, sure enough, the bellow came again. Sid said: "That's Bluey alright, a fortnight early. I shall have to get up." I told him he was not to: sweating like that, it could kill him. Feeling so ill, Sid reluctantly gave way and I climbed out of our warm bed to see if the cow needed help. I hurriedly put on my oldest and warmest clothing, picking up a flashlight on my way out, which I found I did not need as there was a glorious moon lighting up the snow-covered yard. As I entered the cowshed, there before my eyes was our young Bluey with a calf just showing. I soon realized that she was having trouble and was not going to manage to born the calf on her own, although I was experienced enough to know that the calf was coming the right way. I grabbed a rope hanging in the shed, which was used for these occasions, and with great difficulty managed to tie it around the calf's feet in the correct way. Then I waited for Bluey's next pain. When it came, I pulled with a downward movement, as I had seen both Sid and father do, as hard as my strength would allow. Each pain accompanied with the hard pulling showed little advancement in the birth of the calf. Sometimes it even seemed to go back a bit. "If only I had a man's strength," I was thinking, then suddenly, with a mighty push from Bluey, the head was born. I knew we were winning the battle, so long as the other limbs were positioned the right way. After the shoulders were born, the rest was easy and there on the floor was a struggling, wet, slimy, blue, bull calf. I squeezed the mucus from its nose as I had seen Sid do many times, but the next task was beyond me. I had to get the calf into a barrow to wheel it down the yard and into the calf-place, where all the newly-born calves were taken to be dried off and to be cared for until they were strong enough to join the older ones. I tried and tried but I could not get the slippery little animal into the barrow. I thought that, if I turned the wheelbarrow on to its side, I could quickly right it with the calf staying inside, but no, every time it slipped out. In the end I opened the shed door and dragged the poor thing by its front feet down hard frozen snow in the yard and put it in the calf-place. There I rubbed it dry with straw and covered it with large sacks. I went back to see if the mother was alright and there she lay, looking as comfortable as an old shoe.

Thankfully and with a glorious feeling of a job well done, I went back into our warm house, took off my dirty outdoor clothes, washed off the remains of blood and mucus from the calf and crept into bed. It was steaming hot from Sid's fever and gratefully I became warm and comfortable again. As I settled down for a good night's sleep, I said to Sid that I had never seen a cow take things so calmly, for cows usually make such a fuss when their calves are taken away from them. He asked me if I was sure Bluey had lain down again so quietly. When I assured him this was so and I wondered why, Sid answered that Bluey was most certainly going to have another calf and twins nearly always came a fortnight premature. "Oh no!" I cried, "not another one." "Yes," said Sid, "just you wait and see." Sure enough, after about fifteen minutes, there came another bellow loud and clear, so I hopped out of bed, dressed quickly and raced to the cowshed where another calf was showing. I went through the whole procedure once again but the baby this time was a heifer calf. Both were blue like their mother and I always had a special feeling for these two calves which were called Lilly and Larry.

I had only one more experience of borning a calf on my own but this one turned out badly, I lost the calf because I did not remove all the mucus from over its mouth and it suffocated. I thought I had cleared it properly but I had left the slightest thin kind of skin that stayed over the nose and mouth, almost like a thimble on a finger, My only excuse was that the calf was born in a badly-lighted shed and I had not seen it. We were very sorry to lose a perfectly good calf because of such a slight error on my part, but that night Sid had been to a sale of land where he had been the highest bidder for a field. We were so excited at being the owners of a really good bit of land, the first we ever owned. It was around twelve acres and cost eight hundred pounds. Now that same land, because of years of inflation, is worth around twenty thousand pounds.

Our boys were growing into sturdy youngsters and became an increasing joy to us parents. Sidney was never so happy as when he was outside with his father. His keen interest in farming showed itself at a very early age. Young David showed the same keen signs of what he wanted to do, but in another direction. At the very early age of two and a half years he would lie for hours, flat on his tummy, with his elbows on the floor supporting his chin, studying his elder brother's illustrated children's encyclopedia. Grandma Smith, even at this age, nicknamed him the Professor. This came true, for David is now a Professor of French at the University of Toronto and served for five years as chairman of his department.

The time came when Sid and I discussed very lightly the idea of buying a car. Neither of us knew the first thing about cars or how to drive them. We thought we would give about fifty pounds for a second-hand car that would pull a trailer for taking pigs, calves and poultry to market. We were not definitely sure of ourselves or even terribly enthusiastic about the idea, but one Monday morning my brother John told me that a friend of his, named Jack Talbot, had bought a ten-horsepower Wolseley for seventy-five pounds. It had only 11,000 miles on the clock and had not a mark or scratch on it. The car had belonged to a rich lady who owned three cars, including a Rolls Royce. This Wolseley had been used for shopping trips and had never been driven more than forty-five miles an hour. John said not to hesitate, as we might miss it. I always had a sense of a good buy, so I put on my hat and coat and, while John stayed with David, went to see Mr Talbot. He was not in but Mrs Talbot showed me the car; it was certainly everything John had said it was. I asked Mrs Talbot to give us the first chance of buying it. She said her husband had been offered eighty pounds but thought he could probably get more and it would still be a very fair price. It was just after one o'clock when John Talbot drove the car into our yard and invited me to have a test drive. I was making David a new coat and was fitting the sleeves, but John said: "Never mind that. Pick him up, pins and all." So David sat on my knee with only one sleeve in his coat which was pinned in. I was sure the car was everything we could desire, so when we drove back into the farmyard, we sat and discussed the matter. John said he thought it was worth eighty-five pounds and the first to offer that sum could have it. In my excitement I offered him the eighty-five and we shook hands on the deal. Afterwards I felt in a dream. What was Sid going to say at my temerity in buying a car all on my own? It was only a matter of an hour or so before he would be home from market. I was feeling quite shaky and I kept going over and over in my mind just what I was going to say and how to broach the matter. When Sid sat down for his dinner, I did not say anything I had rehearsed at all, but as I gave him his plate, I blurted out: "Sid, I have bought a car for eighty-five pounds." I shall never forget his face. He stood up and exclaimed: "You've what?" I repeated what I had said. Sid fumed: "I never knew such a mad thing in all my life. You've bought a car, you who know absolutely nothing about cars. You must be mad, girl." For Sid this was so out of character, but I was sure I had done the right thing, so I told him to get on with his dinner, as our car was coming at three o'clock and it was nearly that now. Sid had just finished and was still very put out, when this shining car drove into the yard. We both stood at the window looking at it as it came towards the house. We looked at each other and Sid gave me a re-assuring hug and said: "You're right, Nell. It's a beauty." We hurried out to examine the car and John took Sid for a short drive. Within minutes of his return, Sid had made out the cheque and was well pleased with such a classy-looking car.

Now we had a problem of learning to drive. John Talbot said he would teach us when he had a little time. He suggested that, when he had business in Loughborough or Nottingham, we should take our car, with me driving. I still remember the feeling I had the first time at the wheel and driving out of our yard. I asked John to keep his hand on the wheel, as we went through our narrow gateway and made a sharp turn on to the road. He must have had nerves of iron as he made me drive the whole way to Nottingham, but when we reached the outskirts, I refused to drive through all the traffic of the town. When his business was finished, we drove from Nottingham to Loughborough and I managed to drive through Loughborough moderately well. When Sid finished his day's work, a number of friends took turns in teaching him to drive. There was great competition between us to see who would be the best driver. We drove many miles before we took our driving tests, but with petrol at one shilling and two-pence a gallon, the miles didn't matter. Sid took his driving test first at Melton Mowbray. When I asked to be allowed to sit in the back seat, the examiner agreed, so long as I did not speak a word. I should have loved to answer some of the questions on the Highway Code that Sid was making such a hash of, but I kept quiet. Sid had never bothered to learn the Code but I had memorised the whole thing parrot fashion. After Sid passed his test and received his papers, I told the examiner I wished I was taking my test that day. He said I could, as he had a spare hour, so I did and also passed, but I was disappointed not to be asked any questions on the Highway Code. The mind boggles at the ease with which driving tests were taken in those days. Youngsters now have to wait months before a test appointment and the test is very hard to pass.

16 THE SECOND WORLD WAR

On September 3rd 1939 the British people heard on the wireless that we were once again at war with Germany. Immediately farmers were alerted that every ounce of food would be needed and that we farmers would be forced into altering our way of farming. The first compulsory order was to grow sugar beet, a crop many farmers had no experience in growing. The man in charge, whom we called the sugar beet man, lived in Rempstone, a village just over the border into Nottinghamshire, two miles away. He was very strict but fair. He ensured that the acres allocated to the growing of sugar beet were properly grown and gave advice to farmers with no experience of this work. In those days we had no modern machinery and it was terribly heavy work, even for strong men, lifting the beet that grew deep into the ground.

An amusing conversation was heard between two men lifting sugar beet out of very hard ground. First man: "I hate this job, sirry." Second man: "You can say that again, lad, but I tell you what. Every two beet we pull and knock together to get rid of the muck, just imagine that one beet he old Hitler and the other be one of his henchmen and we are knocking their heads together to knock some sense in 'em." First man: "Ah! That be a good idea, sirry. It sure will help a lot. Damn old Hitler, it's all his fault, blast his eyes."

A sugar beet factory was built in Nottingham and the farmers were ordered to send in their crops at a time specified by the sugar beet man. This operation was highly organized, for if one farmer was late in arriving at the factory, the whole work was held up and that farmer was duly chastised.

We also had to plough up a certain percentage of the grassland for crops, which meant the common land and grass verges were once again appreciated and very much grazed by our reduced number of cattle. More pigs were kept, but their diet consisted of almost anything available. Neighbours saved their few scraps and potato peelings, which were boiled and mixed with whey from the cheese factory. When the Wymeswold airfield was established, one farmer fed a whole herd of pigs from the waste he fetched from there. These were the fattest pigs we ever saw, but they were in great demand, as fats were strictly rationed.

Once again, as in the First World War, country people fared better for food than the town people. I learned, as my mother had in the previous war, just what to do with a pig. By law we farmers were allowed to kill two pigs per family per year. Sides, legs and shoulders were all salted down in the cheese vats at the bottom of our cellars. Grandpa Smith, who was an old hand at this job, took charge of this operation. When three weeks had passed, the brine was washed off. The legs, which were now hams, and the sides, now flitches of bacon, were hung on huge hooks from the kitchen ceiling for another three weeks, by which time they were dry enough to take upstairs to the store-room. My mother, Grandma Smith and my Auntie Sheppard, who lived in the next farm to ours, all came to our house to help make the pork pies. We treated this day like a party and we all enjoyed the gossip that went on, while raising the pies on wooden moulds and two-pound jam jars. Once again our friends and relations benefited from each of our pig-killings.

There was a lot of black marketing in the farming industry. We had an animal feed rep call who offered Sid extra rations for our milk beast. Sid thought this was wonderful, not realizing there might be something shady in this offer. I wanted to know more about where and how he could get more than our ration of foodstuffs. The rep, quite unconcerned, stated that sometimes a bag of food was left short at another farmer's place. These odd bags mounted up, so he had a few extra bags to sell cheap. He little realized the avalanche of fury he was about to receive from me. I flayed him with words, saying he would steal from one farmer and sell to another, and I despised him utterly, and so on. Sid was much quieter in his condemnation of such a mean trick. Needless to say, we had no further truck with that gentleman.

I expect we all did a little black marketing, for I remember that eggs were rationed in the towns, but in the country this seemed not to be the case. Anyone was allowed to keep a few hens – I think up to six – without disclosing the number of eggs laid, but these eggs were certainly shared with those who had no way of keeping poultry. During April and May, considered the egg glut time, hundreds were preserved in huge pancheons. I remember that, when our young son David was in hospital, I quite innocently took an egg each for the children in David's ward. It was not until I saw the sister's amazed attitude in accepting the present that I realized just how tight egg rationing was in the towns and even in the hospitals.

During the war farmers were allowed a small extra ration of petrol, but the police frequently stopped cars to make sure they were being used for a legitimate purpose. One morning the village bobby walked majestically into our farmyard and knocked at the door. As he came in, I noticed that he was taking out his little book for notes. After umming and ahing, he at last got to the point and asked me if it was true that my husband had taken a load of Wymeswold bowlers to Willoughby to play in a match. I answered: "Yes, quite true." He ummed and ahed again and wrote in his little book: "Quite true." "Is it also true that your husband had a puncture on the way home?" "Yes," I answered, "one tyre had a puncture." "Umm, umm," he said, and wrote that down, too. I began to see where this was leading, but I kept quiet. "Did you know that your husband was breaking the law, using petrol for non-farming purposes?" I said we both realized that the petrol ration was only for farming activities. In a hard voice he said: "I shall have to report this matter to higher authority." I was simmering inside with laughter, but I kept a straight face and replied: "When you send in your report about my husband, please report at the same time that a certain Wymeswold policeman uses petrol every Sunday morning to take his son's girlfriend three miles to catch a bus to Leicester. Oh, and by the way, Mr Policeman, I didn't know that a pony and float with rubber tyres used any petrol, for that was the vehicle my husband used to take three old men for a game of bowls at Willoughby, since they were unable to ride bicycles." Didn't he look red!

Because of the war all private building was stopped. Father had retired and my brothers, Warner and Bill, obtained responsible jobs helping to build the new aerodrome. This aerodrome took up many acres of Sir Edward Packe's estate, which was situated between the villages of Hoton, Prestwold, Burton and Wymeswold. When the aerodrome was completed, the Wellington bombers arrived, along with instructors who had finished their bombing sorties over Germany. We had one of these instructors stay in our rooms, which enabled his wife to be with him. This instructor was a real hero to my two boys, who listened entranced to his stories of his experiences in the air and his trips over Germany.

Later on in the war, our Wellingtons were among the eleven hundred bombers that bombed Cologne one evening. So often the bombers limped home, only to crash in the fields around the aerodrome. One Wellington crashed in the field opposite my childhood home, out of which struggled an airman alight from top to toe. Most of the boys were killed, yet they were less than a mile from the runway. These old Wellingtons had a sound reputation and were looked upon with awe by people living in the villages round the aerodrome.

Early in the war we bought a heavy road caravan for fifty pounds from a Mr Crossland who lived in the village of Burton. Our two heavy horses, with the help of our strong pony, pulled it out of the frosty ground, on to the road and home. It was parked in the yard while I stripped the inside, painted and decorated it, and installed a new cooking stove, bedding and kitchen utensils. I even put in all the oddments we were using at home and a new dinner and tea service. These I was advised to keep myself, but I refused, as I wanted everything to be nice for the prospective tenants. No sooner was it ready than a council representative came and commandeered it for a family of evacuees from London, who paid a regulation rent of five shillings per adult and three shillings per child. Much to my sorrow, within three weeks my lovely caravan, that I had spent weeks getting in perfect order, was a shambles. Saucepans were burnt and quite half the dinner and tea service was broken. Fortunately, the family soon went home, as did many other evacuees, when the expected bombing of London did not materialize. In subsequent years we let it first to people from the aerodrome, and later to ex-servicemen studying at Loughborough College. All of them were good tenants and became close friends, many of whom still visit us from time to time. The caravan later served as a hen house, then as a store place, and has only recently been demolished.

We also let rooms in the farmhouse as part of our war effort, charging a ridiculously small rent. Again the first letting was a dismal failure. We had cleared out the incubator room, furnished it, making a large sitting room, and rented it along with two large furnished bedrooms to a family of three. The father and son were quite alright but the lady hated living in the country. She called her rooms a hole, abhorred washdays in an outside wash house where she was always letting the copper fire go out, and when her wireless fused the lights, stamped her feet and fumed about "this God-forsaken place". When I eventually obtained an electrician, he told her the fault was her own, as she had fitted the wires wrongly. All she had to do was to keep her room clean and their clothes washed. I did all the cooking and charged them three pounds ten shillings a week board and lodging for the three of them.

An amusing incident took place one breakfast time. When the son was soaking in his tea those hard biscuits we used to buy, his mother gave him a sharp slap across the arm. When he protested that he was only doing what Mr Smith did, she declared: "Never mind what Mr Smith does, you are not to do it, since it is so rude." "Oh well," replied the boy, "you always do it when we are at home, mummy dear." We all tried very hard to hide our amusement at this sally.

After this family had been with us around five months, I began to feel extremely unwell. It was several weeks before I realized I was to have another baby. Sid asked our lodgers to find other accommodation and we were very relieved to see them go. Michael, our third son, was born on a bitterly cold Sunday morning to the sound of church bells. He was a beautiful baby, almost too pretty to be a boy. Lottie was with me during the birth and thought I had got a girl at last. This baby was not planned and Sid used to tease me, saying: "Now which is it, the postman, the baker or the candlestick-maker?"

During the end of my pregnancy with Michael, Sidney and David came downstairs one morning looking like death warmed up. After having no breakfast, Sidney decided he would go to school, but when he came home looking yellow as a guinea, I knew he had jaundice. David, who felt much too ill to go to school, took to his bed and became gradually worse, to the great puzzlement of our doctor. A rash of huge red spots the size of a halfpenny appeared on his body and the skin on his finger-ends peeled off like thimbles. He had a high fever, found great difficulty in moving his limbs, and could not bear even the firelight in his eyes.

At two o'clock one morning the doctor said he must go into hospital. We wrapped him in warm blankets and Sid carried him to the car and sat him on my knee. We sure were a front-seat full – I was eight months pregnant and David's blankets seemed to take up an awful lot of room. That was the worst car journey I ever had. There was thick fog, snowed-up icy roads and the fear of bombers dropping their bombs on Nottingham, but the gods were with us and we arrived safely at the Children's Hospital. Tests were taken for meningitis, typhoid and rheumatic fever, he was placed in isolation, but his illness was never diagnosed, though on Christmas Day he had five specialists examine him. After three weeks in hospital his fever left him and we fetched him home looking like a skeleton. Sidney, who had slowly got better, had missed his brother badly. He even declared that he would never quarrel with him again. This vow he tried hard to keep, but within hours they were at it again. Young David was quick to take advantage of being ill, knowing full well Sidney would not clout him until he recovered.

Oh, how lovely it was to have them together once again! When I went into labour, David went to stay with his Grandma Smith. The very next day he came out yellow all over and thereafter his recovery was swift and sure.

When our baby Michael was three months old, I saw an airman looking at our house very intently. I thought he was admiring the pear blossom covering the walls, which was particularly lovely that year. He smiled and nodded, then cycled away up the lane. Later on, just before we sat down to tea, a knock came at the door and there stood the same airman. He asked me if he might have a word with me, then enquired if our house was big enough to accommo-. date another family of four. "Oh!" I answered, slightly nonplussed, "I'm not sure that I could." I explained about our previous lodgers who had become such a blight on our lives. He quietly took out of his wallet a snap of his family and held it out to me. Even at that one glance at his wife Win, I knew I should like her, and that with a face like that she could not hurt anyone. All this time I had kept him standing at the door. I suddenly realized my rudeness and invited him inside, where he saw Sid patiently waiting for his tea. Apparently Sid and the young airman had chatted to each other up the lane. I invited him to sit down and have tea with us. (I recall that half a home-cured ham was on the table.) After discussing his great desire to have his wife and two children with him, I offered him the rooms we had to spare – a large sitting room with the bedroom above. His wife would have to do her cooking along with me on the huge black cooking range in our living-kitchen.

They came on a month's trial basis and stayed for six months until Arnold was transferred to Iran. We all fitted in peacefully, were extremely happy together and were in tears at our parting. In the following years we stayed with each other a number of times. When I first saw their house in Morecambe, with all mod cons, I realized how well they had made the best of things in a country home, for never did I hear them grumble. When I said something like this to Win, she answered: "Nell, believe me, it was worth it to be together for those six months." As with many other couples, it was a long weary time before Arnold came home.

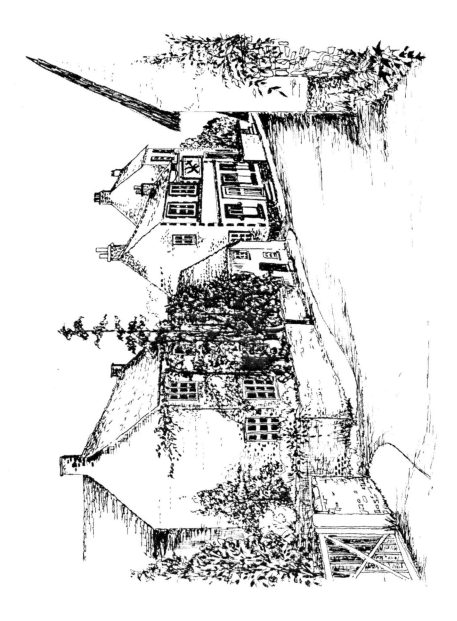

When the bombing of London began and the docks were blazing, we began to worry for my sister Edna and for Sid's Aunt Nan and Uncle Fred who lived near the docks. I knew Edna would not desert her hospital, but I thought Aunt Nan might want to leave, so I wrote to tell them they could have a home with us, away from the bombs, any time they liked. It was not until their house was bombed that they came to us, bringing an old friend who lived with them. Aunt Carrie, Sid's other aunt in London, came shortly afterwards, bringing her only son John, who was thirteen years old. Aunt Carrie lived with Kathleen and John stayed with us. Aunt Nan and Uncle Fred lived with us for nine months, when they were lucky enough to find a house to rent. They moved in with what was left of their furniture and lived out their lives there.

Sad though the war was, we enjoyed the odd outing. Having had officers living with us, we were sometimes invited to their mess parties. And oh, my goodness, what parties they were! Near the end of the war we attended what was, in fact, the airmen's last Christmas party. It was something out of this world, considering that it was wartime. The room was fully decorated and on the central table was a whole half-grown pig with an orange in its mouth. Beside it was a suckling pig, also cooked whole and with an orange in its mouth. These pigs were surrounded by turkeys and every other kind of cooked meats. After we had all had a good look at this magnificent sight, the chefs started to carve slices from this huge assortment of meats. I saw many of the visitors filling their handbags with slices of meat wrapped in their serviettes. The food was there in abundance and it was obvious that it could not all be eaten in one evening. I have never been to a dance before or since where there were such quantities of gorgeous food.

During the war our village social life was practically at a standstill, but there were times when we made our own entertainments. For example, we formed a concert party whose members had the best acting talent we could find. Twice a week we practised in our farmhouse kitchen for around three hours, but at half-time we celebrated with a glass of home-made parsnip wine and a mincepie or jam tart. We performed many plays during the war years which were much enjoyed by the villagers and by friends from the surrounding villages.

There was one play we did where Joy Brown and I were supposed to be chatting at a tea table as the curtain went up. I was supposed to be in trouble with my husband and was telling her all my worries. The opening words of the play should have been hers: "Well, my dear sister, it's time you were going. You must face up to your worries and tell your husband." Unfortunately, for the first and only time in her life, Joy was completely stage-struck and could not get a word out. Realizing her trouble, I took her words and said; "Well, dear sister, I think it is time I went and confessed all to my husband." Joy immediately took the cue and after that everything went fine.

Another time one of the boys, supposed to be a French count, missed out four pages of script. We received no prompting from the back of the stage, but knowing the whole script, I was able to bring the action back to the right page with a little bit of ad libbing, for which the boy and the rest of the cast were duly grateful. The prompter told me afterwards that he had sat behind the stage in semi-darkness and had no idea where the lad had got to.

A party of our drama group went on a tour of the Bourneville chocolate factory, where we were given tea. When we had finished, we had a half-hour's wait for the bus, so we thought we would go through the play we were currently rehearsing. I was playing the part of a foppish young man about town, wearing a top hat and carrying a cane. We were supposed to be at a tea party where I had to say in a la-di-da voice: "More tea, waiter, more tea." To our discomfiture, the factory waiter brought our group another pot of tea. He looked surprised to see our astonishment at the arrival of another pot of tea. When we told him we didn't really want it, he looked at me and said: "You ordered it, Madam, and not in a very pleasant manner either." When I explained to him that we were rehearsing a play, he was very amused and insisted we drink the tea.

At these concerts we were lucky to have Connie Brown who sang several songs with her fine soprano voice. When the concerts were over, we usually held a dinner-party in the farmhouse kitchen, followed by games and dancing. The proceeds from these concerts were given to the Red Cross or to Church funds.

Early in the war I had an interesting conversation with a lady named Miss Disney, who travelled round the villages on a bicycle, carrying a huge suitcase on the back and a smaller suitcase in one hand, while she steered the bicycle with the other. Her father owned and worked a knitting machine, making very strong, warm, hard-wearing socks which were much appreciated by the farmers. She sold these socks along with many other different lines in drapery, Miss Disney was a British Israelite who believed that everything that happened in the world was forecast in the Bible. She prophesied that France would be overrun but England would eventually win after great suffering. She also said that this war would not be the war to end all wars, but that in the last great war we would be fighting with the Germans against the Russians. She forecast that Russia would have a terrible weapon to turn upon her enemies, but that eventually it would be turned on themselves and destroy them utterly. The Caucasus would be termed "the valley of dead bones". Most of her predictions came true and the invention of atomic bombs and other devices makes the rest seem possible. After this war with Russia, she forecast one thousand years of peace. Another saying of hers was that Ireland would be a thorn in our side all the days of our lives. She was a most impressive woman who lived until her recent death in a small cottage in the nearby village of Wysall, ever ready to make Biblical prophecies and still giving music lessons at nearly eighty years of age.

EPILOGUE

These memoirs have stopped during the Second War when I was about half my present age. Much has happened since, too much even to summarize here, but a few details should perhaps be mentioned.

My parents both died at an advanced age, but all my sisters and brothers are still alive. Warner has just turned eighty, but less than ten years ago he was working on the church roof and is still active. My parents-in-law died in their sixties and my husband died of a heart attack at the age of sixty-one, just after we had moved into our new bungalow and chicken farm. Two of my sons are farming: Michael in the family farm and Sidney in another farm in the village. David teaches French in the University of Toronto. After the war I had twins, a boy and at long last a girl. Richard is in personnel management and Lizbeth is in partnership with me in the egg business. All my children are themselves parents and I have fourteen grandchildren, six boys and eight girls. I hope to be a great-grandmother before much longer.

My memoirs for this period have been written and they will be read by my descendants whenever they are curious about family history or want to know something about the lives of the people who appear in the family photographs.

I am lucky to enjoy very good health and still do a day's work that a young woman would be proud of. I thank God every morning when I get out of bed, ready for my work on the poultry farm. I still dislike sitting around doing nothing.